# Praise for *MindShift On Demand*

"Donna Blevins is someone we can all look up to, both professionally and physically!"

—**Zig Ziglar**

"Donna's message is unique and universal. It never ceases to amaze me how right on she is, and how her read on any situation and intuitive sense of people, often are the catalyst to moving people through their blocks."

—**Kelley O'Hara**, Marketing Director
The Bicycle Casino, Los Angeles, California

"I use several of Donna's vivid and empowering MindShift Exercises to set myself up for a more focused, productive, and enjoyable day. I highly recommend her MindSet Coaching for everybody ready to change their 'inner games' and go 'all in' for greater success and joy in life."

—**Marcy Jenkins**, MBA
BestFitStrategist.com

"What's most helpful is that I now have a way to put stress from daily life aside and relax, that way I can loosen up instead of tensing up, which used to affect me negatively."

—**Mark Castrovona**

"You turned my world around in 2008, Donna! It was the first time in years I felt I knew what to do and got my ducks in a row without feeling scarcity, distracted, or disappointed in myself. All thanks to your coaching!"

—**Kelly Rudolph**
PositiveWomenRock.com

# MINDSHIFT
## *ON DEMAND*

QUICK *Life-Changing Tools*

# MINDSHIFT
## *ON DEMAND*

Donna Blevins, PhD

*Relativity Publishing*
*Inverness, Florida*

**Relativity Publishing**

1108 E. Inverness Blvd., Suite 611, Inverness, FL 34452

Relativity Publishing books are available at special quantity discounts to use for incentive-based fundraising, for healthcare advocates to encourage wellness, for premiums and sales promotions, or for use in corporate training programs. For bulk sales or to book the author as a speaker or executive coach, please email info@DonnaBlevins.com

**Disclaimer:** The author is not a medical doctor and is not suggesting you stop any of your medications or shy away from your doctor's instructions in lieu of the MindShifting tools within this book.

The contents are based on the author's personal experience and research. Your results may vary, and will be based on your individual circumstances and motivation. There are no guarantees regarding the level of success you may experience. Each individual's success depends on his or her background, dedication, and desires. The author and publisher assume no responsibility for your actions or results.

ISBN 978-1-944070-00-7 (Paperback Edition)
ISBN 978-1-944070-01-4 (Hardcover Edition)

**Library of Congress Control Number: 2017952122**

1) Self Help 2) Motivation 3) Sports Psychology

First *MindShift On Demand*™ printing, October 2017

# Dedication

For my mother, Mama Peggy, who, at 91, still lovingly calls me "papoose," even though I'm six foot five.

For my husband, Gregory, who, at five foot three, shores me up— no matter what—and is one of the few people I look up to.

For my "heart" dog, Herman, who wakes me up in the middle of the night and helps me reset my heart.

For my sponsor-partner, Genesis Gaming, creator of the Bravo Poker LIVE app, who stepped up with confidence that what I say truly matters.

For my coaching clients, coaches, dear family and friends, who kept insisting, "Just write it down... NOW!"

# Contents

# READ ME FIRST

The brain is the most powerful tool you own, yet most people fail to understand it.

Imagine the possibilities if you could harness the power of this magnificent biological supercomputer! MindShift On Demand will teach you to tap into this potential and be the best version of yourself: Confident, authentic and in control!

If you're looking for tactics that put you back in control of your emotions, instead of being pushed around like you're a sissy, you've come to the right place. If you're feeling overwhelmed and looking for ways to shift yourself mentally out of fear, anxiety, and worry, consider this:

*Shifting your mindset is as simple as grasping the gearshift knob in a vehicle and smoothly shifting from one gear to the next... if you know how and when to shift.*

Please understand: Life is a journey full of twists and turns... complete with potholes, road blocks, traffic jams, dead ends, and freeways. Your body is the vehicle; your mind is the driver.

Sometimes your mind gets away from you and becomes a bad driver. Unfortunately, your unconscious mind can sabotage you. However, your conscious mind, along with MindShifting, can put you back in the driver's seat.

How you view what's going on and what you do in that moment either puts you in the driver's seat where you can create the life you want, or leaves you an unwitting passenger.

## WHY MINDSHIFTING IS ESSENTIAL

When people approach me for help with shifting how they're thinking, a common thread that surfaces revolves around a loss of confidence, self-doubt, and failure.

Using the tools presented in these pages, 9 out of 10 people have taken the wheel and upshifted their lives to the next level. They've broken losing streaks, quieted nerves and anxiety, released fears, regained self-confidence, and reestablished self-esteem.

Within these chapters, you'll discover a dozen MindShift Exercises™ that can work for anyone—anyone who wants to excel in whatever they do—whether with family, in relationships, in business, and in life.

Read all the way to the end and learn time-tested techniques to:

- Perform at the highest levels under pressure
- Take control of your emotions instead of letting them control you
- Replace negative self-talk with powerful confidence to attract success
- Strengthen your body by strengthening your mind

## HEY! WINNING IS IMPORTANT!

Everybody loves to succeed, and failure quite frankly sucks. However, when we focus only on succeeding and reaching our goals, we frequently second-guess ourselves and lose sight of our prime objective—to make correct decisions using the information we have at hand.

Our main purpose in every facet of life is to make correct decisions... not just some of the time... not just most of the time... but every time.

Yet, in whatever we do, we constantly make decisions based on incomplete information. We never know it all. But here's the kicker: when our must-know-it-all mind insists on waiting for all the facts, we paralyze ourselves.

We over-analyze facts until we're stuck in a "do-loop," crashing like a corrupted computer and failing to take any action at all.

Worse yet, after taking too much time to weigh all of our options and then finally acting, we often discover that our window of opportunity just closed. We failed to take our foot off the brake and missed our chance.

Here's the point. There's a fine line between acting too quickly and acting too slowly. At the same time, life can throw sand in our gears. Even after we make a 24-karat-gold correct decision, situations constantly change.

Life evolves. A spot-on decision we just made might become wrong in the next instant because conditions continually transform around us.

We must gear up and shift our mindset in harmony with the flow— being mindfully responsive rather than unconsciously reactive. MindShifting gives you the tools to do exactly that, by fine-tuning your perspective and creating the life you want.

## EMOTIONAL AGILITY

In the middle of any situation, when your emotions flair and grab you by the scruff of your neck, you can't just say, "Please excuse me. Give me half an hour while I recompose myself, meditate, and calm down."

Any mind is a terrible thing to ignore. You need to get over emotional imbalance without delay and refocus your attention. You need to learn emotional agility, which is truly a priceless life skill.

Since your perspective defines your reality, you must find your sweet spot.

Once you know how and when to shift your mental gears—and take suitable action—you've intentionally put yourself firmly in the driver's seat. You are then fully prepared to safely cruise along life's highway, regardless of what's around the curve or over the next hill.

## MY THANKS TO YOU

As special thanks for grabbing this book, I've put together a FREE audio collection of several of my MindShift Exercises™. As you play the recordings, listen to my voice and imagine that I am speaking directly to you. That is exactly my intention—to speak from my heart to yours. You can access the audios and graphics on my website: **www.DonnaBlevins.com/mindshift**

## LET'S GET STARTED!

In the first chapter, you'll discover how I could have lost everything in one life-shattering moment. Instead, I found the keys to controlling my mind and healing my body. Instantly, I geared up, tested the limits, and proved that MindShifting absolutely works. Just think of me as a self-acknowledged guinea pig.

Read on, and let's get started shifting together.

# CHAPTER 1
## STROKE OF GENIUS

Lightning flashed and struck inside my head. In my mind's eye, I was falling from the sky in slow motion. Time distorted and slowed. Floating like a feather, I felt like the landing took around twenty minutes.

CRASH! Thud! Suddenly, I hit the floor in a split second.

Searching for words, I could only blurt, *"$#!*!"*

A few moments before, I stood up from my computer, whining to myself, *"It's not working. No one cares what I write. Who will even read it?"*

Staring at the words on my computer screen, I emphatically barked, *"I want something to PROVE my MindShift Exercises™ work! I want PROOF... NOW!"*

Literally, I stomped my foot like a brat and lightning sparked. It felt like a mule had kicked me in the head.

Lying on the floor, I sighed and thought, *"Ahhhhh, be careful what you ask for."*

The result was a massive stroke caused by my dysfunctional heart. You might think I'm nuts calling my stroke a gift, but it clearly was.

What occurred inspired me to shift my mindset rather than empowering the stroke and worsening its effects. In real time, I was given the opportunity to shift away from physical trauma and mentally observe in lieu of engaging and magnifying the results.

Think about the possibilities when you're blindsided by life. If I had stressed out, focusing solely on, and *owning*, my physical condition as it happened, brain damage could have moved rapidly along the scale—from possible to probable to permanent.

Even though the blood clot came from my out-of-rhythm quivering heart, I must admit I still suspect my foot stomp started the process. It gives me a chuckle when I envision sitting astride a motorcycle, repeatedly stomping down on the kick-start. When the engine revs, the cycle lurches forward like a rocket, and I'm launched backwards. I clearly forgot to shift the transmission into neutral.

Despite the source, my stroke opened a door to absolutely prove mindset shifting works. I got the proof I had been asking for!

The clot completely blocked blood flow to the central part of my left-brain, which is the area of the brain hardwired to control speech. On top of that, we're cross-wired. The left brain controls physical parts on the opposite side of your body—including the right side of your face, writing with your right hand, taking a step with your right foot, etc.

Since blood carries oxygen and fuel to every cell in our body, block the flow and it's just like turning off the gasoline to a car. The engine stutters and stops.

The stroke caused the central part of my left brain to suddenly quit. You might say that segment of my brain "flat-lined."

My healthcare professionals voiced concerns that I was most likely permanently broken. I could hear them clearly, but I was unable to speak except for two words.

That day was Halloween, October 31, 2013.

## WE CHOOSE OUR MINDSET

What I'm giving you is an honest, unfiltered first-person view of what went on inside me, what lead up to the event, and what went on around me. When I crashed to the floor, I had a choice. I could either remain in fear and anxiety, or I could detach from it. Instantly, a voice popped in my head as an internal conversation began.

The following is a brief replay of the dialogue between my Inner Coach and me:

*Inner Coach:* "Look, you asked for it! You created a platform to prove your MindShifting works. Now get up, put your shoes on and get on with it."

*Me:* Weakly, I replied inside my mind, "I'm terrified. I'm afraid of what just happened."

*Inner Coach:* "Engage your energetic radar. You have the power within you to notice when your energy is out of sync and to shift."

*Me:* I took a long deep breath and sighed, "Ahhh... Okay. Give me a moment. Let me settle.... Energetic radar engaged." I felt the shift.

*Inner Coach:* "Now detach. Rather than feed your fear, detach."

*Me: "Detach?" I whined again, talking back. "That's so easy for you to say!"*

*Inner Coach: "Of course you know how to detach. You teach people how to shift. Back up your talk with your actions. You have control over how you act rather than re-acting. Now, get on with it!"*

*Me: "Hmm, that is interesting...." Slowly, I used one of my MindShift tools. I inhaled deeply, smiled, did the simple step-by-step MindShift, and exhaled. "It's done. I'm detached from the fear. Now, I am the eyewitness."*

*Inner Coach: "Good. Now get up and act."*

There you have it. That's exactly how MindShifting works by using simple steps.

When you're shifting your mindset, you will frequently have a conversation in your head. With continual practice, the process of MindShifting becomes natural and automatic. You can become unconsciously conscious.

You will be able to shift your mindset almost immediately—if you take intentional, focused action to re-train both your mind and your brain.

## WE CREATE OUR REALITY

You might be thinking, *"Seriously? How can I possibly create my reality?"*

Here's my point:

*When we're unaware, we speed through life on autopilot.*
*Unconsciously, we crash into one barrier after another.*
*Everything seems out of our control.*

Willfully shifting our mindset requires awareness, sensitivity, and the courage to act. Once we know how to shift our mind's focus, it's swift and easy to change gears. We become the driver rather than remain the clueless passenger.

During my stroke, I located my mindset gearshift, became aware, and detached from fear. It was smooth going—clutch engaged, shift, clutch released, and cruise.

The gearshift enables the driver to directly synchronize with the vehicle. The exact same thing happens when we willfully shift our mindset.

That's life. I was now the driver, in sync and ready for the road. The journey began.

## MY JOURNEY

*"Ask and ye shall receive."*

I asked for and received an arena where I could prove my MindShift Exercises™ do work. Astonishingly, I was suddenly aware of a truth I had overlooked:

> *MindShifting can positively work on BOTH your mindset and your physical body, including your brain!*

As a mindset coach, I had a flaw. I had missed the roundabout connection between mind and body in my own life, and also within my coaching clients.

Prior to this life-altering experience, I had primarily focused on correcting emotional imbalance rather than paying attention to the body. Before I crashed to the ground, it never occurred to me that shifting our mindset energy could be used to physically heal our body. I asked for proof while I was writing this book and **ZAP!** I received way more than I anticipated.

## MY POINT OF VIEW

During my stroke, communication with the outside world was distorted and one-sided. Even though everyone thought I was offline, I was 100% mindful inside.

I remember. *Every. Single. Tiny. Detail!*

Have you ever received a phone call when you heard the caller but the caller could not hear you? The other person stayed on the phone for a fleeting time and hung up while you kept saying, *"Hello! Hello! Can you hear me? CAN YOU HEAR ME NOW?"*

When staff at the hospital assumed I was unaware, they huddled together at my bedside, talked about what was going on and what they expected. They were within earshot range and I heard everything clearly. Inside my mind, I completely understood what they were saying.

Since the hospital caregivers thought my mind was disconnected, they lowered their voices but stayed where they were, quietly debating with each other. They did mastermind brainstorming and spoke quickly among themselves, searching for a solution. They believed I was unable to hear or understand.

Even though I was unable to speak, I heard crystal-clear. When one sense is disabled, another sense is frequently improved. As an example, some blind people have intensified hearing.

Since I was effectively voiceless except for my 2-word vocabulary, my hearing was amplified. The volume inside my head was booming.

Because I didn't want to offend anyone, I struggled to change the first word out of my mouth. Everyone nodded when I muttered, *"Donna,"* and chuckled when I repeatedly yelped, *"Crap!"*

The joy I experienced during the process may amaze you. I clearly remember what everyone said and I am deeply touched by my care. I know their names, their faces, and I have connected with many of them after my recovery.

When doctors make a prognosis, they may be attached to the outcome of that prediction. Doctors are trained to diagnose and then to take action. I've wondered if it's possible when a diagnostic result is firmly expected by doctors, if the result they anticipated will likely happen.

Teachers have told me that when they expect a class to perform in a certain way, that is what they get. No more, no less. They usually get what they expected.

From my point of view, rather than hold onto the doctors' forecast, I had detached and become the observer. *My energy was focused on healing rather than fearing. That's one of the things MindShifting allows us to do.*

## OVERVIEW OF THE JOURNEY

**Day Zero, Halloween:** My husband and mother rushed me to the nearest hospital's ER. I was directly airlifted to UF Health Shands Hospital, which is the University of Florida teaching hospital in Gainesville. Without hesitation, they took me to the brain cauterization lab and located the clot that closed off the left, central part of my brain. I was completely awake, aware, and at ease. Because I was motionless, they thought I was unconscious and in a coma. The procedure took about an hour.

**Day One, Friday:** I spoke about 20 words. Well, I sort of spoke. I was stuck on the first syllable of most words.

Inside my mind's eye, I was holding a remote control, similar to the one you use with cable TV. My simplified, internal remote has several large key buttons: *Delete, Cancel, Pause, Next.* Whenever someone said anything that I preferred to shift away from, rather than "owning it and becoming it," I pressed a button to change that channel.

The speech therapist said, "It will take at least 90 days to recover your voice. However, 6-9 months will likely fly by before you can speak fluidly. Possibly, you might remain permanently speech-impaired."

*Cancel. Delete. Next!*

I scored 5% on the speaking test. The speech therapist went on to say, "There is no need for me to come back to see you next week. It will take you a very long time to recover."

**Day Two, Saturday:** While my husband drove back home to check on mom and the pups, I spent the day by myself. The staff was kind but never attempted to verbally engage with me. They dashed in and out, silently doing their duties.

At least once an hour, I rang the call button needing my water refilled. When they came, I held up the empty water container. They probably thought I was mentally challenged and kept pouring the water down the drain.

What I'm going to relate to you may seem too "out there" and not evidence-based. However, I did promise to give you my unfiltered, first-hand look at what went on inside me, and that's exactly what I'm doing.

And yes, I do understand that a stroke affecting a part of the logical left brain often awakens the creative right brain. However, I am both logical and creative by nature.

The following is how Day Two progressed.

During the waking hours, I was busy in my internal brain gym retraining myself how to talk. To speed up the process, I added self-care and body movement to the mix. I drank water constantly. Every hour, I walked around the wing, smiling and nodding to everyone I saw.

To start, I asked myself a question, *"How can I easily regain my ability to speak?"*

The first thought that came to mind startled me, *"Stop being frustrated."*

Consciously, I set aside the frustration that arose when I couldn't find a word. Rather than thinking I had lost a word, I simply thought, *"I've temporarily mislaid that word."* Changing the way I was thinking, along with the words I said to myself, felt like genuine self-forgiveness.

My next question was, *"Where did the words go?"*

The answer surprised me. I envisioned there was a long row of large, multi-drawer filing cabinets full of words inside my brain. Someone had pulled out all the drawers and dumped every file on the floor.

All my words existed, but they were disorganized in a mountain-high pile on the floor. I was confident that once I located and filed the words back into their proper folders, I could easily say them.

Throughout the day, I jabbered incoherent words to myself while I moved my body this way and that. I made a mental list of the words I needed, just like you might do when you go to a foreign country. How do I say hello? What do I say to order food? How do I ask where the toilet is? How much is the meal? Where is the market?

Using my word list, I closed my eyes and visually located a particular word file in the pile. The file folder I imagined morphed into

3-dimensional word figures. I liked that. Some were block letters. Others were italics. Many had different fonts.

Once I found a word, I would spend awhile mentally holding the word in my hands, turning it over and over; feeling the texture and form of the letters, their weight and temperature. Mentally, I heard myself say the word as I drank water and breathed in deeply and slowly.

With my eyes closed, I physically moved my hand and arm to pull open the appropriate drawer. I alphabetically filed the word back into the drawer, and then, closed that drawer.

Ponder this: I was having a reunion with each word, and making each word a part of me once again. Could such visioning rewire the neural pathway from my word file to my mouth?

This I know for a fact. Everyone learns and heals differently. Yet, whatever we want to become, we speed up the process by staying in positivity and light, rather than regret, hatred, frustration and owning the illness.

**Day Three, Sunday:** At the crack of dawn, I pressed the nurse call button. When the nurse arrived, I was sitting on the side of the bed, feet dangling. Smiling from ear to ear, I breathed in deeply and slowly said, "Hi, I'm Donna Blevins-Weitzel. I'd like to talk about what's been going on inside my mind and where you think I've been."

The nurse froze. Holding her breath, she began blinking like she was blinded by a bright light shining out of the darkness.

I began chattering and felt like I was having a pep rally. Everyone on that wing came running. As I related my experience, they listened with their mouths hanging wide open. The doctors were stunned and said they had never witnessed anyone with this type of recovery.

Throughout the day, dozens of hospital staff came by my room and said, "Uh, we heard you had a stroke?"

I welcomed them with open arms. "Come on in! Let's talk."

**Day Four, Monday:** I called the speech therapy office and asked for the therapist to "come by Donna's room." When he tested me later that afternoon, I scored 95%. Shaking his head, he said, "This is the first time I've ever seen such an incredible recovery."

**Day Five and Six:** As they closely monitored my heart medication around the clock, I napped and chatted with the staff. I noticed how 12-hour shifts brutally drained the staff's stamina and altered their state of mind.

> *FACT: Negativity surrounds you in a hospital and infects your energy field unless you consciously protect yourself.*

Negative energy affects you the same way when you're surrounded by throngs of people—in bustling cities, in busy malls, riding packed subways, or elbow-to-elbow in the workplace. Think about how you feel when you are engulfed by everyone around you.

When I mentioned I was a coach, most every caregiver at the hospital asked, "What do you coach?" Smiling, I replied, "I'm a Mindset Coach," and watched their reactions.

Even though they didn't sigh out loud, I felt some moan when they said, "I sure need a coach but don't have time."

I went on, "I help people shift their mindset. We do have a choice how we respond despite what life tosses our way."

One nurse almost shouted: *"I DON'T have a choice! There's so much I MUST DO!"*

"I completely understand your workload in healthcare," I went on. "I'm here in the hospital as a patient. I see what's going on. I feel it. But, you do have a choice. I sense you are completely neglecting self-care, just like I did. Airlifting me to your hospital got my total attention."

She replied, "So, what can I possibly do?"

My response was, "You can put *The Egg* on and energetically safeguard yourself."

Shrugging, she said, "Okay, but that sounds really odd. How do I do that?"

## WHAT HAPPENED NEXT

After sharing my MindShift Exercise™ *The Egg* with her, I watched as she began insulating herself from the overpowering negative energy around her.

I was happily surprised that she immediately engaged in the process. At the same time, I was delighted when she experienced a positive, energetic shift.

Her energy shift was outwardly apparent—the change in her body language, the tone in her voice, and her facial expressions.

As I shared *The Egg* technique with other staff members, the way they physically carried their bodies literally transformed in front of me. They loved the simple process and told me they would keep *The Egg* on and use it in all areas of their lives!

## WHAT IS THE EGG?

*The Egg* revolves around consciously protecting your entire energy field by deflecting negativity surrounding you. In the '70s, I was introduced to the concept.

Since then, I customized the method which has become sacred to me. You'll find the steps in a later chapter.

Within that chapter, you'll also discover a liberating twist that frees your mind. Rather than the necessity of remaining consciously aware of *The Egg* every single moment, we can set it and forget it. However, we must check in, from time to time, for repair by scheduling routine maintenance for our own personal *Egg*.

**Day Seven:** In a very short time frame, doctors, nurses, and techs said this was the first time they had ever seen a startling recovery like mine. They said it was a miracle.

Checking out of the hospital, I encountered the senior resident who headed the team that had greeted me in the ER. It was the first time I had seen her since they airlifted me to the hospital. When I said hello with her name, she looked up, furrowed her brow, and said, "Who are you?"

I smiled broadly and remained quiet. She suddenly blurted out, "Mrs. Blevins?" My reply was, "Just call me Coach."

We talked for more than an hour, and she accompanied me as I left the hospital. She had never seen anyone completely recover from a stroke which had closed off the blood flow to the left central brain.

It's gratifying to get concrete proof of the positive effects of conscious MindShifting. *I asked for proof and got it!*

## HOW MINDSHIFTING PRODUCED VERIFIABLE RESULTS

After I crashed to the floor, the effect of consciously and constantly shifting my mindset produced dramatic, positive changes in my body... instead of leaving me disabled.

Every single challenge in our life provides us with opportunities to shift. Regardless of when trials surface—whether at work, at home having fun, during a relationship, dealing with aging, being a caregiver, or fighting an illness—life just happens.

To prepare for each day, I use the following intention: *"To stay in the moment, make correct decisions, and remain unattached to the outcome."*

The truth is, I now live life differently. I trust I can see opportunities that arise, take calculated risks by acting, and capitalize on the situation.

We always have a choice. How we respond to what's occurring alters our reality.

## COACH DONNA'S INTENTIONS FOR YOU

My intentions: To show you how to take control of your thoughts and shift your mindset at a moment's notice, to present new strategies for living your life at home and work, to support you in interacting with healthcare professionals in a socially conscious manner, and for healthcare professionals to connect and talk with you rather than at you.

Open your mind and prepare to fill your ToolBox with MindShift Exercises™. Now is the right time.

## BOOK OVERVIEW

Here's a quick overview of what follows in the book.

You're about to discover twelve quick and easy ways to shift to a champion mindset. Along the way, you will naturally customize your own MindShift ToolBox™ to fit who you are and where you would rather be.

To provide concrete proof that MindShifting works, and to validate that shifting your mindset is effective, I'll be sharing other people's positive results as well as my own.

Hopefully, you'll be able to use what you learn to heal your body and improve your health, be more in control of your life, and shift your energy to joy rather than sorrow, anger, and regret.

## UP NEXT...

The next chapter gives you a quick taste of MindShifting with your first MindShift Exercise™, called *Gear Up*.

In any part of life, continual practice anchors habits. Just become aware of what you practice.

# CHAPTER 2
## GEAR UP (MSE 1)

You come first. Regardless of your responsibilities, you must first focus on you. Since your body is your vehicle, self-care is like auto maintenance.

That might sound silly, but when you ignore changing oil in your car, the oil will break down over time, lose its effectiveness, and no longer properly protect your engine.

Ignoring self-care results in a buildup of emotional residue, just like sludge in an engine. You may lack energy, gain weight, prematurely age, or suffer with depression. You know what I'm talking about. Many people have "been there, done that, too."

Although an oil change is preventive maintenance, a tune-up is what will allow you to run at a higher level, accomplish more, and require less energy. Working with a mentor or a MindShifting coach helps to make sure you are running on all cylinders at your peak performance.

Heck, your mindset might only need a few simple tweaks, much like an engine with easy-to-fix timing issues—adjust a little this way, then that way, until you find the sweet spot. Just don't wait for the "check engine light" to come on!

It's time to gear up, focus on self-care, and change the oil. You matter. You deserve your undivided attention. You can get results when you take action and engage in the process. As a result, you will end up with tools you can easily use.

## LET'S BEGIN MINDSHIFTING

Your first MindShift Exercise™ is *Gear UP*, which is an **ATOM, A Taste Of M**indShifting, a tiny sip you can savor like fine wine.

Let me play with some words. Envision this exercise as the *Atomic Effect* to shifting your mindset: *Simple triggers produce explosive results.*

*Gear Up* is a quickie, a *MindShift Mini-Treat™*. LOL! Sounds like a new vehicle to me, the *MindShift MINI™*.

When I started chuckling, in my mind I could just hear the 15-second commercial, *"Design your own MindShift MINI™ and shift your mind in a moment. Schedule a test spin you'll never forget. Sit down and buckle up! You deserve MINI-me time!"*

The moment I wrote down that sound bite, I was curious and searched the Internet for the Cooper MINI car. I had never looked at anything about that car before. Face it. At 6-foot 5-inches tall, who would?

The following is a selling point used by the car manufacturer, *"Stop by to learn how to design your own MINI over 10 million different ways."*

What a coincidence!

You can design your own, personal, MindShifting tools a million different ways as well. I believe customizing automatically occurs within each person. By continually practicing, you become the co-creator of your MindShift ToolBox™.

Consider this. The more you use the MindShifting methods you discover in these pages, the more they become yours. They will become UNIQUELY yours. Our mind is a vast, unexplored territory with endless possibilities.

Taking repeated action anchors the habit of MindShifting, just like learning how to fluidly shift a manual transmission. Practice generates muscle memory. Repetition trains your body and your mind while strengthening their bond.

Your continual actions fine-tune each MindShift Exercise™ based on your point of view. You add your own flavor and individualize the process based on your life experience.

## PHYSICALLY CHALLENGED?

Since visioning or visualization is powerful, even if you are physically challenged, your body-mind-spirit interface will still work. If you are unable to move, lack a limb or are paralyzed, or if you cannot otherwise physically engage in any MindShift Exercise™, as I guide you, just imagine in your mind's eye that you are physically moving.

If you are fully functional physically, but you're in a situation where you prefer to shift without publicly drawing attention to what you are doing, shift your attention to your mind's eye view.

By envisioning you are using particular muscles to move your body in a specific way, your mind will believe you are literally, physically moving. This may take practice.

## GROUND RULES:

1. Since engaging in the process by closing your eyes helps, avoid driving a vehicle or operating heavy machinery while doing many of the MindShift Exercises™. You will know which methods are safe to use while driving.

2. While physically driving a vehicle, if you find yourself stressed, overwhelmed or mentally fractured, find a safe place and pull over. Pick a method that you discovered in the pages of this book and shift away!

3. In reality, I believe I have automatically used self-forgiveness before each exercise, even though I left that step out when I wrote down many of the methods. Consider using forgiveness as your way of engaging in any process.

4. I also believe gratitude belongs within each exercise. Giving thanks is a powerful tool that helps us heal, energizes us, and can change our lives for the better.

Now, it's time for a test drive. Let's gear up for the shift.

## PRACTICE SHIFT: GREASE THE GEARS

Even if you understand how to manually shift gears, indulge me for a moment. The purpose is to create a connection and awareness between the mind and body. The shifting process inside your mind is like driving a vehicle with a manual gearshift.

Slowly read the steps below and imagine you are driving a car.

Physically move your body as you read the gear-shifting steps, or imagine you are doing so. Concentrate on feeling the clutch-shift rhythm. Rather than expecting to feel a shift, consider this a practice run where you engage your body while activating your mind.

**Gear UP:** Clutch. Shift Up. Release Clutch. Accelerate.

**Cruise:** Clutch. Shift Up. Clutch. Cruise.

**Gear DOWN:** Brake. Clutch. Shift Down. Slow. Release.

**Stop Safely on Level Ground:** Brake. Clutch. Shift to Neutral. Release. Idle. Foot softly remains on brake.

When I shared the clutch-shift insight with coaching client Debbie, she said, "I just experienced a MindShift! I'm going to start using the gearshift. I can picture that in my head and use it to shift to where I want to be."

When editor Val read this chapter, she said, "Once physically engaged in this exercise, I was mentally invested. After a split second, I was driving like a pro. Because I physically went through the process, my mind was in it, and there was no herky-jerky motion."

Searching the Internet for stick shift, I liked these results: "Driving a manual transmission takes some training, but can be accomplished by pretty much anyone who puts their mind to it. Driving smoothly takes some knowledge and finesse."

**NOW WHAT?**

Since you've gotten into the gear-shifting rhythm by physically moving your body, or visioning that you are, the process of becoming the driver is simpler than you might expect. No fancy, intricate actions here.

Taking control of your mind and putting you back in the driver's seat can happen quickly. Once you grasp the three simple steps for

*Gear Up*, you can close your eyes, take a deep breath, engage your body, and become the driver in a few seconds.

However, rather than an instant shift—which *Gear Up* can literally become—I suggest you take one full minute going through the process. Consider the following three steps as your way of taking a mini vacation.

## "GEAR UP" DETAILED STEPS

### Step 1: Visualize your gearshift.

Take a moment. Close your eyes and take a slow deep breath. Imagine you are the driver sitting in the driver's seat. Own that feeling. You are there now that you are aware.

### Step 2: In your mind's eye, as you clutch and release, see your hand fluidly shift the floor gearshift on your right.

Physically, reach your right hand over and go through the motions of shifting gears. Move your left foot up and down as you shift with your right hand. Feel how comfortable you are in the driver's seat and how smoothly you shift.

The mindset gearshift allows you, the driver, to orchestrate harmony in your life instead of magnifying discord. Right now, seeing yourself as the driver shifting gears puts you in full control of your mindset.

### Step 3: Embrace your reality shift.

You have now shifted and changed your point of view. Rejoice in the fact that you are consciously your mind's driver, rather than remaining an unconscious, reactive passenger.

**Bonus:** At the end of each chapter containing a MindShift Exercise™, you'll find simplified steps that help you remember and recall each exercise, along with an abbreviated QuickShift™ to speed up the shift. Then, in the Appendix at the end of the book, you'll find the MindShift Rolodex containing all twelve methods for quick reference, along with a short recap of each method and its corresponding QuickShift™.

## "GEAR UP" AT-A-GLANCE

1. **Close your eyes. Take a long, slow breath in and out. Visualize your gearshift.** You are the driver sitting in the driver's seat. Your floor gearshift is to your right.

2. **Continue intentionally breathing slowly. See your hand fluidly shift the gears as you clutch and release.** Move your hands and feet as you run the gears. Notice how comfortable you feel in the driver's seat and how smoothly you're shifting the gears.

3. **Embrace your reality shift.** You are now your mind's driver.

Tip: **Want a faster shift?** Simply taking one slow, long breath and seeing yourself as the driver can bring you back to being completely aware and back in control of your mindset.

## "GEAR UP" QUICKSHIFT™

1. **Slowly take one deep breathe as you close your eyes and visualize you're sitting in the driver's seat.** Hold your breath as you reach over and intentionally grasp your gearshift.

2. **Slowly exhale. In that one single breath, you've become aware.** By doing so, you've experienced a true reality shift. You are now back in control of your mind in a mere moment.

## PROGRESS CONFIRMATION

Since you've experienced your first MindShift Exercise™, *Gear Up*, you've had a taste of MindShifting and begun the journey. You're on the road to learning a dozen methods in this book.

At the end of each chapter containing a MindShift Exercise™, you'll find a customized, unique Progress Confirmation sentence that gives you a glimpse at how that technique might help you.

Take a moment right now to help anchor *Gear Up*. With conviction, intentionally say the following aloud:

> *"I am taking control of my mind now that I've learned to shift with Gear Up and have become the driver."*

## UP NEXT...

Chapter 3 is about our mind-body connection and how that interaction works. Now, let's get on with it together. I'll ride shotgun as you drive.

# Chapter 3
## The Mind-Body Connection

As the caregiver for two heart patients, my husband and my mom, I was also the primary breadwinner. I rushed to tend to everything except me, neglected my self-care, and in 2011, my heart went haywire.

My plate was full. I was juggling caregiving with running my mindset coaching practice and developing an online training business, including membership sites. In my spare time, there were accounts to balance, dogs to tend, groceries to buy, cars to maintain, and a house to keep.

The dogs and people were well-fed, and the car ran like a top. Sure, if you looked closely, you might find last season's bugs clinging to the headlights. The accounting bookwork and the house... well, let's not go there.

If I painted the entire picture of what I was doing, I'd convince you that I was a lunatic. Yet, I kept feeling like I was just not doing enough. You may have experienced something similar.

Frustrated, I posted on my Facebook timeline, "I need a wife." The flurry of responses startled me. Could there possibly be that many people experiencing the same sort of madness?

Yet, I thought I couldn't *afford to slow down*. I simply ducked my head and lunged forward, like a crazed bull.

My husband says I'm like one of those robot vacuum cleaners. Point me in a direction, and I go furiously until I hit a wall. Then, I bounce off the wall, turn around, and take off at full speed.

I was about to crash into a different kind of wall. By now, you may have guessed that stubbornness is one of my greatest flaws.

In order to finish a new training program, which I had planned to launch in Las Vegas the summer of 2011, I started mainlining coffee. I knew I could get it done by the deadline *if only* I could stay awake, glued to my computer.

Without moving from my chair, I sat at my desk for hours. Convinced I would get up after I finished *just one more task*, the tension continued to mount in my body.

Finally, the stress took its toll on my wellbeing and my body rebelled. My heart started misfiring. The doctors put me in a no-fly zone, and I was forced to cancel my trip to Las Vegas.

Traitor! My body had betrayed me. I learned a new definition for the word *deadline*.

When my cardiologist told me I needed to meditate, my mental knee-jerk response was immediate: *"Ri-i-i-i-ight."*

Experience told me that I had neither the patience nor the time to do traditional meditation. I suspect you know exactly where I'm coming from.

But, I had to do something. What could I do?

The doctors said my heart condition was genetic and told me, "You just have to live with it."

My mother has the same heart condition. So did her mother. In fact, my grandmother died a lingering death from an avalanche of strokes that resulted from her malfunctioning heart.

I kept undermining my mindset and thinking, *"Oh my. Am I destined to be a victim of my heritage? Is THIS my future?"*

Even when you're unable to change your physical condition, you can change the way you think and respond. Rather than react and continue to fuel a physical challenge, you can change your mindset. Your perception—the way you view what is happening right now—creates your true reality.

In lieu of stoking an emotionally-charged fire, I could detach and become the observer. Yes, I could. I knew I could. However, at that point, I was energetically consumed and began to own my heart disease, and my condition got worse.

Looking back, it's clear that I was blatantly reacting to my illness rather than being responsive and making a change in my mindset.

The more you talk about and believe you're sick, the sicker you become. Your ailment can devour you.

## YOUR BODY IS A BATTLEGROUND

What's the biggest problem when crappy stuff happens to us? We automatically focus on the wrong things: *Our mistakes. Our troubles. Our illnesses.* That's what I did with my misfiring heart.

What are the results? We create more of the same: *More mistakes. More troubles. More illness.* That's precisely what happened with my heart.

When my heart started misfiring in 2011, I slipped into fear. The more fearful I became, the faster and more irregular my heart started beating. I was creating more of the same, a real Catch-22, which was certainly a self-defeating course of action.

At first, I didn't consciously realize I was afraid. I was unaware and simply reacting. I was not thinking. My emotions were in control of me, fanning the flames of anxiety.

In a flash of absolute clarity, I recognized that I was not simply afraid. I was terrified. At that moment, when I finally realized I was in fear, I knew I could do something about it.

I had been reacting and focusing on my helplessness. The more I thought about it, the more the fear grew. Fear had become a monster that consumed me. As it did, my heart beat more erratically. I panicked and stress overwhelmed me. I thought I might die.

Interestingly, it's the same synergy at work in every part of our life. Fear is one of our worst enemies.

Other people can sense your fear. They're like tigers catching the scent. They start stalking you and pushing you around. You feel helpless and slip into a victim mindset.

When you become the victim, you give your power away to the bully. I was giving fear the power over me.

The moment I realized my fear was keeping my heart out of sync, I became empowered.

The wake-up call literally helped me bring my heart out of its irregular heartbeat and back into natural rhythm by taking action and MindShifting.

## THE HEART RHYTHM RE-SET PROCESS

Near the end of 2011, doctors told me they could do a physical intervention to correct my irregular heartbeat.

They would go in through the arteries in my groin and snake instruments up into my heart. It's one of the ways they access the heart during a cardiac cath, a procedure when they look at the heart's circulation, open arteries, and install stents—small metal tubes that act as scaffolding to provide support and help keep your heart arteries open.

By accessing my heart this way, they would freeze and potentially kill the cells in my heart that were misfiring. Supposedly, that would fix the rhythm problem.

During the procedure, the technology they use to pinpoint the misfiring cells is similar to the GPS for vehicles. It was very sophisticated and I fully expected that it would be a success.

The operating room was ice cold. Frigid is a better word.

They plastered my naked front and back with adhesive rubber rectangles about two by four inches. Then they connected wires to each of the patches and ran them to huge machines.

As I sat there on the operating table with my teeth chattering and my body shivering, I thought, "This looks like a scene out of the movie *The Matrix*."

The rubber rectangles were so cold, I shook uncontrollably as I counted backwards from 100 and trailed off... ninety-nine... ninety-eight... ninety-seven... ninety-...

When I woke from the procedure, it seemed like no time had passed. The moment I woke up, I was thrilled to see the doctor standing at the foot of my bed. I was eager to hear his report.

My hopes crashed with his first words, "Your procedure was unsuccessful." (He must have skipped bedside manner class in medical school!) In disbelief, I asked, "Why?"

The doctor responded, "Because you have a ticklish heart. Every time we did something, it triggered something else."

It was obvious at that moment that they had shocked me multiple times during the procedure. My chest felt like I had been kicked by a pack of mules. I wondered if that was usually what happened during such a heart procedure.

I sighed and thought, *"Maybe it's just in my genes."*

The doctor turned to the nurse standing beside him and said, "I am concerned about her. If her heart does not reset by eight o'clock tonight, we're going to have to do something radical."

My inner voice shouted, *"For goodness sake, it's my heart that malfunctioned, not my hearing!"*

Imagine how that might put you in a state of fear. To add to my feeling of vulnerability and fear, I had to remain still and lay flat on my back for several hours. I felt confined and powerless.

After the procedure, they had put large clamps around the top of my legs to put pressure on the arteries to ensure I didn't bleed out. They reminded me of clamps you use to glue pieces of wood together.

It's a helpless feeling when you're restrained and unable to move. You are at the mercy of others.

I asked the nurse to get me up as soon as possible. When they finally allowed me to sit up, it was around 4:30 that afternoon.

As I sat in the chair, my mind cleared and the clouds lifted. In that moment, I discovered that I was resonating fear. I could plainly feel the vibration of fear. If you've ever felt or tasted fear, you know what I mean.

At the same time, I felt my heart beating out of rhythm. They call it arrhythmia (a-rith'-me-a). Humph. Before, I couldn't spell arrhythmia without a spell checker; now I had it.

The reason I'm telling you these medical terms is so you understand the significance of what happened next.

Since I'm very sensitive to the energy in my body, I could feel the top part of my heart *quivering* rather than beating naturally.

Each of the top two chambers of the heart is called the "atrium." Doctors call the quiver AFib, which is short for Atrial Fibrillation.

At the same time, I knew that the two bottom chambers of my heart, the ventricles, were throwing extra beats. They call those beats PVCs, or premature ventricular contractions. I could feel the thumps of the extra beats... thump-thump... thump-thump... thump-thump.

As my heart quivered at the top and threw these extra beats at the bottom, I felt like a rag doll someone was madly shaking. The fear mounted.

All of a sudden, I shouted to myself, *"Crap! I AM AFRAID! I'm feeding my fear!"* (By now, you probably have guessed "crap" is one of my favorite words.)

In that moment, I was elated because I believed I could shift my focus and positively affect the way my heart was beating. The instant I became aware and acknowledged I was someplace I did not want to be, I was able to take action and shift my energy.

Using my Signature MindShift Exercise™ (which you'll learn in the next chapter), I forgave myself for being afraid, disconnected from my fear-based energy, and started shifting to where I wanted to be.

That was a good start, but, more action was required. I rang the nurse's buzzer and quickly asked, "When can I walk?"

The nurse said that I could walk right then. I asked her to bring me something to hang the bags on that were still attached to my body. She brought me a wheelchair with a tall metal rod on one side.

I remember thinking, *"If they just put a flag on the rod, they could find it when someone leaves the chair in the parking lot."*

That silly thought was welcomed. I chuckled softly to myself.

I asked the nurse to point me in the direction of the heart monitor station. She told me to go around the corner to the left and stay on the green carpet. I had to stay in range so they could receive the signals from the portable heart monitor I was wearing.

When I walked up to the monitor station, I said, "I'm Donna Blevins. Please pull up my monitor screen."

The nurse looked at me like a puppy dog cocking its head from one side to the other, trying to figure out what you're saying. As she pulled up my screen, I said, "My heart's out of rhythm. I'm in AFib, and I'm throwing PVCs every second beat. Correct?"

She blinked a couple of times and looked at me again with the head tilt. I asked again with a smile, "Is that correct?"

"Yes," she tentatively said and paused. Her voice went up on the end of the word yes, which went perfectly with her tilted head. It sounded like she was asking a question rather than answering one.

I said, "Fine. What time is it right now?"

She responded, "5:15."

"Good," I said. "Please write that time on a note pad. When I come back in a little while, I want you to record when my heart goes back into normal sinus rhythm."

She looked at me and did another one of those back-and-forth puppy-dog head tilts. She wrote 5:15 on the small yellow note pad to the right of her keyboard.

Now I'd like to tell you what happened next. It still gives me goose bumps whenever I talk about the experience.

When I turned away from the nurse's monitor station and started walking down the hall, I was feeling empowered. With each step I took, I snapped my fingers and said, *"Beat... Beat... Beat..."*

I walked at 60 steps per minute while simultaneously snapping my fingers at 60 snaps per minute. As I began to smile, chills surged through my body. I was taking back control of my body with my mind. I was using the pulsating energy of my mind-body connection.

As I walked around the hospital wing on the green carpet, I was smiling, snapping my fingers and speaking the beat. Once I felt my heart slip back into natural rhythm, I walked back to the monitor station. I no longer felt the vibration of the top part of my heart quivering and I stopped feeling the thumps of the bottom part of my heart throwing the extra beats. My heart was purring.

When I walked up to the monitor station, I said, "I'm Donna Blevins. The last time I was here was 5:15, correct?"

She looked at the note pad to the right of her keyboard and said, "Yes, it was 5:15."

With a broad smile, I asked her to pull up my monitor screen and tell me what time my heart reset and went back into regular rhythm. She blinked in disbelief as she looked at the screen.

Her mouth fell open slightly before she began speaking, "Yes, you were here at 5:15. Your heart went into normal sinus rhythm at 5:21."

## SUMMARY

There are two keys to MindShifting. First, realizing the power of your body-mind connection, and second, knowing how to activate that connection.

One Twitter follower tweeted me @BigGirlPoker: "Thank you Donna! Your MindShift Exercise helped me deal with stress and clear negative energy from my body."

This book is a toolbox full of how-to MindShift Exercises™. Regardless of your situation, you can use these tools to make your life immediately better.

## UP NEXT...

To discover exactly how I shifted and reset my heart, read on. In the next chapter, you'll learn your second MindShift Exercise™ *Hmm... Isn't That Interesting?*

# CHAPTER 4
# HMM... ISN'T THAT INTERESTING? (MSE 2)

In this chapter, you'll find your second MindShift Exercise™ *Hmm... Isn't That Interesting?* This is my signature method, one which you can use to shift your mind and body out of fear, and then, to a safer, healthier place.

Why start with shifting away from fear? All our problems are rooted in fear. That might be self-evident to you. At the same time, you might have a knee jerk reaction, just like I did. When I first stumbled onto the concept while surfing the Internet, I originally reacted, *"Nooo! I am NOT afraid!!"*

Sure, we're afraid of things outside of us that threaten our safety. The moment I realized that fear contributes to the vast majority of mindset problems, I reacted physically. My mind-body connection experienced a ripple effect, speed-shifting through the gears.

As I glared at the following words on my computer screen, *"All your problems are rooted in fear,"* I caught a glimpse of my face in the mirror on my desk. I looked like a startled, scared kid.

Constantly using a mirror might sound self-indulgent to you. For me, I've been using mirrors to observe myself and see what my face is saying. It's been a way for me to become a better communicator, and I wish I had used the same approach more often when I was in sales.

How do people see me? What does it look like I'm thinking and feeling and doing? What clues am I unconsciously giving off? Do I look serious and truthful?

Let me draw you a picture of how I physically looked when I read, "All your problems are rooted in fear."

My eyebrows were down and together, lips narrowed. In a flutter, I raised my eyebrows and upper eyelid while tensing my lower eyelid. That particular flashing facial reaction was a fear-to-anger micro-expression. I was fearful as I became angry.

What was my fear?

Likely, I feared that I was not good enough. On cue, I became angry at the thought.

I'll go into facial micro-expressions in another book. For now, just consider that all your problems might be rooted in fear.

Fear of loss. Fear of not being good enough. Fear of failure. Fear of letting go. Fear of being a victim. Fear of the unknown.

From your perspective, consider this: *MindShifting just might be your Fear Tonic™ remedy.*

## THE KEY

My health challenges since 2011 have given me multiple opportunities to practice and refine my *MindShifting Collection*. In the moments just after my stroke on Halloween 2013, I was able to shift away from fear, gear up, and prove mindset-shifting works.

Looking back, I now believe the key to healing from the inside out is to anchor MindShifting as a natural habit.

Consider this: You might experience a positive healing effect on your body by intentionally shifting the way you are thinking.

The following exercise combines imagination, subtle body cues, and self-talk to shift your energy in real time. That's right: *Real time. Right now. In an instant.*

You might be wondering: Does taking action move you from being negative to completely positive in one step? Rarely.

Making that big of a shift in your mindset is unrealistic, just like going from dead stop to the highest gear in a vehicle in one single motion. Shifting your mindset, and taking control of your mind and your life, is a journey, taken one step at a time.

Think about a real-time app that many people regularly use to get from one place to another. The system responds to input immediately and then reacts to a steady flow of new information without interruption. I use it all the time.

What do you think that is? Yep, you got it—Google Maps on your smartphone or whatever type of GPS receiver you use in your mind.

Shifting your mindset in real time can be as fast as shifting gears in a car. MindShifting helps you to:

- Shift your mood
- Upshift your energy
- Fluidly carry out day-to-day tasks that might ordinarily be stressful

MindShifting helps you control emotional shifts. As a direct result of integrating the methods into your everyday life, consciously practicing them helps to make them stick and become natural habits.

## THE MINDSHIFTING PROCESS

**Overview:** This exercise has seven simple steps that help you shift away from fear quicker than you might expect.

The process may also help you shift away from pain, remorse, guilt, self-judgment, and loss of love. In reality, this method helps reduce the intensity of negative energy.

First, I'll explain how to rate your feelings before and after you step through the method. This creates a feedback system, which tells you how well the method is working for you.

A friend on Facebook wrote: "You've done a wonderful job of laying out the steps for your MindShift Exercise *Hmm...Isn't That Interesting* and I like the fact you break up the paragraphs into one or two sentences. The simplicity makes following along easier for me."

Take some time to prepare yourself to MindShift. For a moment, feel your body-mind connection. Then begin. Simply put, just breathe.

### Get Ready

Step into your left brain, right now, and ask logic to come along for the ride. In order to gauge the effectiveness of shifting your mindset, you want a number that rates how you feel when you start along with another number that rates how you feel when you finish. The difference gives you very simple statistics—how taking a specific action scored. How quick and effective was this particular method?

Once again let me say, rather than once-and-done, MindShifting is a step-by-step process. It does not matter how fast or slow you go as long as you just keep going.

## How to "Rate It"

When you're in physical pain, your healthcare provider will ask you to rate your pain using the pain scale of 0-10. Zero is no pain, 10 is the worst. After a procedure, your healthcare team will again ask you to rate your pain. The result gives them clues. How effective was the technique? What changes might they have made?

The pain scale is meant to render a more objective way to look at pain, even though your point of view is subjective. Then again, that's life. Our reality is subjective. How we see life through our personal lens is uniquely our view.

Use the same 0-10 scale to rate how you are feeling before and after you do the MindShift Exercise™. I'll give it a name. Let's call it your *Mindset Scale™*. Some of the exercises warrant using such a scale.

You decide. You're in charge. You are the driver.

## MINDSET SCALE™

**Baseline:** Before you start MindShifting, how do you feel when you bring a negative situation to mind? Rate it from 0-10.

**Finish line:** How do you feel immediately after MindShifting? Rate it from 0-10.

**Shift Result:** The difference between baseline and finish line.

Did the method work? If so, how well? If not, what else might be happening?

While speaking at a live event in October 2015, I added "Rate It" into the process for the first time. Before we began, I asked the audience to raise their hands. There was a wide range of baselines from 6 to 10.

After we finished, I asked the audience members to again rate how they felt. Many people dropped 2 points. One young woman yelled out, *"I went from an 8 to a zero!"*

## DEFINE YOUR BASELINE

Once a thought, feeling, or circumstance comes to mind, first rate how you feel, just like you would score pain. Zero is nothing. 10 is the worst.

Take your time reading through each step. Enjoy the method. It works.

Let's begin.

## "HMM...ISN'T THAT INTERESTING?" DETAILED STEPS

### Step 1: Forgive yourself.

The moment you realize your mind is in a place where your emotions are in control, the first step is to forgive yourself for being there. You might snap at your partner, be impatient with a co-worker, or become highly agitated by an innocent interruption.

### Before you proceed with forgiving yourself, rate it.

Where are you right now? How do you feel? Rate it from 0-10.

In your personal life, you might be in a relationship that is well worth your effort to repair, or you might have stayed in one too long and refused to let go. Someone might have unjustly taken advantage of you, or you might have unjustly devalued them.

In business, you might have suffered an unexpected grave setback, and now you have less mental energy to help regroup. Consider taking stock of the situation and using this method to rebound.

Regardless of what just happened, you're feeling powerless. You might feel like you screwed up, or that it's your fault. You might feel like the situation is simply unfair, or that you failed to listen to yourself. You knew what to do, but you ignored it.

I want you to realize a simple fact: *You are your own worst enemy.*

When we recognize we are someplace that doesn't serve us, our inner dialogue often intensifies the situation. Our subconscious automatically begins answering any question. Consider the answer when we ask ourselves, *"Why do I always think these crappy thoughts?"*

Whenever you hear words in your head that tell you, *"I'm doing something wrong,"* it's time to take action.

Questions like these give your subconscious mind programming language that reinforces your negative life scripts:

- *"Why do I keep doing this crap?*
- *"Why do I keep shooting myself in the foot?"*
- *"What's wrong with me?"*

The first thing you must do when you realize you're in that negative place is to applaud yourself for the awareness and then forgive yourself for being there. Yes, I said *applaud* yourself when you recognize you are saying negative things to yourself.

*Why? Because in the very moment you understand you are in a negative place, you become aware.*

Awareness and forgiveness are two of the most important parts of MindShifting. Rather than blame or condemn yourself for feeling the way you do, release the blame and forgive yourself.

You might find it challenging at first to forgive yourself.

Let's face it, few of us were taught how to forgive ourselves as children. Most role models show us how to judge and belittle, rather than accept and forgive. Television sitcoms are a perfect example.

I put self-forgiveness under the heading of a learned skill. Many of us were conditioned to ask forgiveness from a deity, but we were not taught the importance of self-forgiveness.

It's easy to see how destructive a judgmental attitude is in personal relationships, but we overlook how damaging self-judgment is to our own state of mind.

I suspect you've been judged by someone close to you—a parent, a partner, a child, or a co-worker. There is nothing more demeaning than being judged. It feels bad. Really, really bad.

On the other hand, a religious person seeks forgiveness without judgment, and that feels good. That goodness is the feeling you create within yourself.

Judgment produces guilt and reaction. As you pull inward and your energy constricts, you close and shut down.

Fortunately, forgiveness opens you up, is accepting, and allows growth. So what if you screwed up? That's part of being human.

**Step 2: Give it a form and name it.**

If you're a very literal person, this step might give you pause. That's okay. You'll get there. Hang with me.

# CHAPTER 4: HMM... ISN'T THAT INTERESTING? (MSE 2)

Close your eyes and think about the emotion or situation that's bothering you. I'd like you to give it a form by turning it into a 3-dimensional object. In your mind's eye, see it clearly.

You might imagine a person or monster. You may recognize the object, or it may look like something you've never seen before.

Don't worry. You can't mess up. Whatever you're thinking of, go with that visual.

You might find it helpful to say, *"Show yourself."*

Or ask, *"What do you look like?"*

Regardless, see it now. Command the object to show itself. Remember, you are the boss.

When the emotion or situation is an intangible, all-consuming thing, we try to grab it. Our thoughts seem out of focus.

If you struggle seeing a form and it fails to show itself, that's okay. Just, try this: In your mind's eye, imagine you are looking at a white board. Now, write a few words on the board that describe what's going on. You will be able to see those words in your mind.

When the emotion or situation takes form, or when you write a few words that describe it, that emotion or situation now has boundaries. And, its power weakens.

*Your pain is no longer just out there surrounding you, illusive and undefinable.* Once you imagine the frustration as an object, or see your words that define it, then that "undefinable thing" now has boundaries and literally starts to shrink and become smaller. In an instant, the circumstance has less power over you, and then you begin to take control.

Alternate method: If a name doesn't instantly come to mind, that's okay. Try asking, *"What is your name?"*

If nothing jumps to mind, make one up. It doesn't matter what the name is. The practice of naming gives you the upper hand and begins to put you in control. You are taking the wheel.

Using this exercise when resetting my heart, I saw a dark red, cartoon heart. The top part was quivering and the bottom part was jerking like a crazy animation.

There was a gnarly-looking monster looming all around my heart with big teeth and slimy drool coming out of its mouth. It was growling and my heart was quaking in fear. The name was easy. I simply named it "The Fear Monster."

**Step 3: Step back and look at the object.**

Once named, the third step is to step back and look at the object. In your mind's eye, take one step backward. The moment you step back and look at the form you've created in your mind, you've put distance between you and that emotion, that feeling, that thought, or that situation.

When you step back and detach your focus, you get stronger. What you are observing continues to shrink and get weaker. It is no longer out there, all around you, overshadowing and encompassing you.

What you observe starts to literally change before your very eyes. When you step back, you disconnect your energy and become the observer. You detach and stop feeding and fueling the emotion, the situation, or your conflict.

Even though you stepped back in your imagination, you have directly activated your *body-mind connection*. Your body is unable to tell the difference between imagined actions and true physical engagement.

Just remain in that head space for a moment and feel the comfort and safety of being detached. As you look at the object with detached interest in your mind's eye, the object continues to shrink and become finite.

## Step 4: Say, "Hmm... isn't that interesting?"

The fourth step is to say aloud, *"Hmm... isn't that interesting?"* End the phrase as if you are asking a question.

When you're in private, you can say it aloud. When you're in public, say it silently to yourself, or the people around you might wonder what's so interesting.

You now have fully become the observer. You are simply noticing the form you created. You are no longer invested in that emotion, that thought, that feeling, or that situation, nor are you feeding it. You have totally separated so that "it" is no longer a part of you.

In that instance when you step back and disconnect, you have become the observer. You have successfully shifted your mental gears.

## Step 5: Look up and to the right.

The fifth step is to open your eyes, look up and to the right. Pause briefly.

This step uses a subtle body movement, which also helps to shift your energy. At the same time, you further activate your *body-mind link* by making this ever-so-slight move.

By looking up and to the right, you access the right hemisphere of your brain. You tap into your personal creativity.

## Step 6: Pivot your entire body to the right, 45 degrees or to 10 minutes on a clock.

Pivot 45 degrees to the right and continue looking up slightly. When you pivot your body, move your feet to the right as well.

If you're sitting down, shift your feet and pivot on your behind. While standing up, turn your body and your feet. When you pivot your body, you are using more subtle body cues to shift your mindset.

Know this now. Your body-mind connection is completely activated.

### Step 7: Ask, "Where would I rather be?"

Lastly, ask yourself, "Where would I rather be?"

That's all you need to do. Just ask. You've asked your subconscious to take you where you would rather be. There is no need to answer consciously. Your subconscious will do the rest.

You've sent your subconscious mind the programming code that begins rewriting your old scripts.

### Now you are at the finish line. Rate it.

Where are you right now? How do you feel? Rate it from 0-10. How has your *Mindset Scale*™ changed?

## A CLIENT SHARES HIS EXPERIENCE

One of my coaching clients is a software engineer, who said, "I think of your MindShift Exercise as a quick and easy way to download and install new software, reformatting my unconscious mind!"

My response was, "True. That is exactly what you are doing! You are downloading code that the subconscious mind uses to rewrite the underlying software."

He chuckled and went on, "Your MindShifting Exercises are effectively code modifiers for your unconscious mind."

I responded, "I like the way that sounds but, from your point of view as a software engineer and computer programmer, what exactly is a *code modifier*?"

From a different viewpoint, his initial response was intriguing and very interesting. His latter part touched my heart and told me that I was doing exactly what I was supposed to be doing:

> *"A modifier is a code that doctors use to describe a medical procedure for billing purposes. If the appropriate modifiers are used incorrectly or forgotten entirely, the result is lost revenue for the doctors and might trigger possible billing audits. The biggest challenge for doctors and staff is staying up-to-date because the code modifiers frequently change."*

> *He continued, "For everyone, life continually changes. For me, forgiving myself for forgetting or screwing up has dragged me down into a deep, dark hole. I repeatedly blamed and judged myself while remaining focused on what I did wrong."*

> *Then he went on to say, "Rather than finding the lessons and getting on with it, I would often crash like a computer, get stuck, and be unable to reboot. Donna, your MindShifting Methods continually modifies my underlying mental code and effectively keeps my code up-to-date."*

> *"They help me forgive myself, stay mentally mindful, detach and observe, all without the fear of losing and becoming less than. Thank you, Coach. Your MindShift Exercises have literally saved my life!"*

If you ever think you need to dive deep and fix what is broken inside your mind, think again! When something keeps rearing its ugly head, you may only be a few degrees out of alignment.

All you might need is a gentle shift to change your perspective and stop shaming yourself. Many people have added "Hmm..." to their go-to MindShift Toolbox™

### "HMM...ISN'T THAT INTERESTING?" AT-A-GLANCE

**Rate It Before:** Where are you when you bring a situation to mind? How are you feeling? 0-10?

1. **Forgive yourself.**

2. **Close your eyes, name it.** Give the emotion or situation a form & name it.

3. **Step back & observe.** Look at the form.

4. **Say, "Hmm... isn't that interesting?"**

5. **Open your eyes.** Look up & to the right.

6. **Pivot 45 degrees to the right.** Continue looking up.

7. **Ask, "Where would I rather be?"**

**Rate It After:** Where are you now? How do you feel just after completing the exercise? 0-10?

**Your Shift:** What is the difference between your before and after rating? How has your *Mindset Scale*™ changed?

### "HMM...ISN'T THAT INTERESTING?" QUICKSHIFT™

When stress, conflict, frustration, or anger arises without the luxury of stepping away for two brief minutes, take two intentional breaths paired with subtle body movements.

1. **Take a deep breath, smile, nod slightly, and say, "Hmm... isn't that interesting?"** In the moment you become aware, you detach and stop fueling chaos. If you are in public, "Hmm" to yourself by clearing your throat and think the words.

2. **Take another deep breath, smile, and continue nodding as you look to the right and ask, "Where would I rather be?"** You have given your subconscious mind a well-crafted question to begin shifting on a deeper level.

## PROGRESS CONFIRMATION

Since you've experienced your second MindShift Exercise™ *Hmm... Isn't That Interesting?*, you are well on your way. It's time to intentionally say the following aloud:

> *"I am creating the life I want, now that I have become the detached observer with 'Hmm...Isn't That Interesting?' and asked the 'Where' question that delivers code modifiers to my subconscious mind."*

## UP NEXT...

In Chapter 5, you'll find one of the most powerful truths I discovered throughout life's challenges. You'll also learn how you can literally reverse the current of your mind-body connection, and what that means.

# Chapter 5
## About-Face

Before we move forward, I want to reinforce the foundation we've already built. Let's dig deep into the underlying reasons how, and why, our mind-body connection works, and what exactly it means to reverse the current.

If you already know the fundamentals, feel free to jump ahead, scan or skim.

However, I recommend you stay with me. You might come across some unique concepts. Some took me more than 50 years to unearth.

When my heart-monster surfaced, the year was 2011.

Back in the hospital room before the walk-and-reset, I had taken very specific actions. When I realized I was in fear, I used the specific MindShifting process I shared in the previous chapter, *Hmm... Isn't That Interesting?*

The process enabled me to disconnect from the fear, become the observer rather than the victim, and move forward to where I would rather be—calm and at ease. Here's how that happened.

## REVERSE THE CURRENT

Think of *our mind-body connection as a fluid, moving, living current,* just like electricity or water. In fact, our thoughts are transmitted by electrical impulses through the cells of our body, which is over 60% water.

Our brain functions—including thought and memory—depend on access to abundant fluid. Sources report our brain has more water than the rest of our body, upwards of 70-90%. We must stay hydrated to keep our mind-body connections functioning at their peak.

Since our mind affects our body by way of our mind-body link, we can reverse that current and use our body-mind connection along with subtle body movements to positively impact our mindset.

Imagine that reversing the current is similar to flipping the toggle on a light switch. However, rather than "on/off," *we're reversing the direction of the current* so that the actions of our body can effectively change our state of mind.

With very little repetition, subtle body movements become cues that are anchored in our subconscious. We can use them as *triggers and pattern interrupts* to shift our mindset swiftly.

**FACT: Our mind-body and body-mind connections are intertwined. Rather than existing in a state of isolation, one continually affects the other.**

At first, this might seem abstract; however, it is quite real. Let me graphically explain how both our *mind-body and body-mind* connections flow seamlessly into each other.

This is a mind game turned into physical form. The object is to create a visual image of how your body and your mind fluidly flow into each other without interruption.

In your mind's eye, I'd like you to see a fascinating, geometric oddity called a Mobius strip, named after a nineteenth century German mathematician. It has only one side that flows into itself. Let me explain.

Imagine taking a strip of paper and connecting the ends. This creates something that looks like a ring or a belt.

Now, imagine what happens if you *twist only one end of the strip before you tape both ends together...*

You'd have a 3-dimensional object with only one side—a circular hoop with the intriguing quality of having only one surface, and only one edge.

When I first came across the Mobius strip, I blinked my eyes in disbelief.

## PROVE IT

To experience this phenomenon for yourself, take a strip of paper about 14-inches long by 2-inches wide. Give one of the two ends a single twist and tape the two ends together.

Now, take a pen and draw a continual line on the paper ring without lifting the pen off the paper. Amazingly, you will eventually reach the beginning of that same line where you started. There is no separation between the outer and inner side of the ring. Without lifting your pen from the paper strip, you have drawn on both the top and bottom sides of the paper strip.

*Hmm... isn't THAT interesting?*

That's how your state of mind works in combination with your physical well-being. One flows into the other without a beginning or an end. They are continually affecting each other. That's the synergy of both your *mind-body and your body-mind connections* at work.

## THE SHIFTING KEY

Here's a key to how MindShifting works: *You literally reverse the current of your mind-body connection, and then, you use your body to shift your mindset.*

If that sounds very simple, well, it is.

Evidence of how your mind affects your body is all around you. When you're sick and feel bad, *stinkin' thinkin'* can literally make you sicker.

Bring to mind a sick man, who walks around with a black cloud hanging over his head. Every word out of his mouth is dark and ugly. His gloomy state of mind hinders his healing process.

The opposite is also true. An uplifted mindset can heal our soul, our spirit, and often our bodies. Even when our bodies remain broken, we are happier and more at peace as a direct result of our elevated state of mind.

*This is our mind-body connection at work.*

## HOW YOUR BODY-MIND CONNECTION WORKS

You've probably heard the old saying, "Laughter is the best medicine." You might even have read about a person who healed an incurable disease by watching reruns of the old television show *The Three Stooges.*

That's a simple example of how our *mind-body connection and body-mind connection* work together in harmony.

If you haven't considered this concept before, let me break the belief down into components that might seem curious. You might even come across some unique concepts I've added, revised or updated.

## LOOK AT THE BODY-MIND CONNECTION

Assume you see something that your mind perceives as laugh-out-loud funny, something which causes your body to laugh. When your body laughs, you make specific laughing sounds.

You move your facial muscles in specific ways—your lips turn up, you open your mouth, and the muscles around your eyes laugh. Air rushes out of your lungs as you laugh. If you laugh hard enough, your shoulders move up and down rapidly. You might even bend over slightly as you laugh using your back muscles.

Laughter positively affects the way your body feels as it uplifts your mindset. This is an example of reversing your *mind-body connections and enabling your body-mind link to affect mindset change.*

When multiple body parts are activated with feeling, the impact on your mind is powerful. Laughter is a highly-charged feeling.

You use a lot of body parts when you laugh: your voice, your vocal cords, your lungs, your chest muscles, your facial muscles, your mouth, your tongue, your eyes, your shoulder muscles, even your back muscles.

It might even include your arm muscles, your hands, and the sense of touch as you slap someone on the back.

Clear scientific evidence exists and shows that laughter literally changes the chemicals in your body. In fact, just by smiling you alter the chemicals that affect your brain.

Search the Internet for 'laughter heals the body' and see what pops up. That is your body-mind connection at work creating a *shift*.

Consider the energy and the symbiotic relationship between your body and your mind.

In short, you can harness the power of your body-mind connection so that you can shift your mindset from negative to positive. This shift takes very little time and can even happen in an instant.

In the moment you become aware that your mindset is tilted like an out-of-balance pinball machine, you can either stay there or shift.

You do have a choice—either continue to sabotage yourself, or take the wheel and shift the way you are thinking.

## HABITS HELP OR HARM

Both positive and negative thinking, as well as good and bad behaviors, are *habits*.

Habitually thinking and acting a particular way is deep-rooted in our subconscious and can genuinely alter our DNA. Either way, good or bad, you are the boss, the dominator, the alpha.

You've probably heard someone say, "It's no big deal. It's just a habit."

That's nonsense!

Habits are directly *helpful or harmful* to our mind-body connection. When bad habits negatively affect our mindset, our life suffers, and our body recoils.

Whatever we consistently do on a daily basis literally turns genes on or off, just like a proverbial switch.

Bad habits become a high-performance rocker switch that turns off good genes while turning on bad ones. This opens the door for bodily damage and disease, addictions, mental challenges, as well as long-term stress.

Allowing bad habits to remain without shifting can literally damage your physical body and potentially kill you.

Even worse, when you allow your bad habits to remain and mutate your DNA, you pass on your modified, downgraded DNA to the next generation.

## TIME TO ACT

Hopefully, by now you've grasped the essence of why and how shifting your mindset can potentially transform your life. It's time to get off your butt and shift.

About-face. Rather than look at your journey as a long haul, amend your travel guide.

Set aside 10-minutes-a-day to anchor one positive habit at a time by consciously MindShifting. Pick one MindShift Exercise™ and play with that one for a week. The following week, choose another one and shift away.

Reinforce your DNA. Depending on where you are in life, enriching your gene pool might be an interesting concept.

Think of yourself as a work-in-progress rather than needing repair. Or, if you've been around for a while, see yourself as a classic, vintage car being restored from the wheels up!

## UP NEXT...

In Chapter 6, you'll find a super-quick preparation for shifting your mindset. Your next MindShift Exercise™ is *90-Second Shift*, similar to skillfully driving a race car. Read on and discover that when we breathe, inhaling can trigger one part of our brain, while exhaling a particular way does much more than you might expect.

# Chapter 6
## 90-Second Shift (MSE 3)

In this chapter, I'll introduce you to your third MindShift Exercise™, *90-Second Shift*. But first, let me take a quick detour. Think of the next few paragraphs as a bypass on the interstate, one which helps you avoid getting stuck in rush hour traffic.

You may have some questions arise as you read this book. That's a good thing. When your mind jumps to a question while you're reading, you are involved in the process. At the same time, you're digesting the content and considering the possibilities.

As questions come up, jot them down and continue on. Writing down questions effectively frees up your brain's ability to move on without getting stuck. Too much spinning around in your mind is like the overload of a computer's RAM (random access memory), which is the place a computer performs tasks.

When we have too many programs open on our computer, too much processing is going on. Computers traditionally freeze and lock up. The only way we can proceed on a frozen computer is to do a forced reboot—a complete shutdown by holding down a particular key, then restarting the computer all over again.

Logging your questions clears your mind. Writing down your queries keeps you away from potentially experiencing mental gridlock.

Yesterday at lunch, one of my book editors showed me a couple of pages with check marks everywhere. When I asked her to explain, she smiled and said, "I write down questions as they spring to mind while reading. When you later answer the question, I go back and check off the question."

Read on. It's time to find answers to your questions.

## WHAT IS THE "90-SECOND SHIFT"?

This method is a MindShifting Tool™ that works alone, by itself, as well as in conjunction with other techniques. I want you to think of the process as a gentle reboot rather than a computer's forced reboot.

Believe it or not, without consciously knowing it, you are already naturally and automatically doing the fundamentals of this exercise. What am I talking about?

Yep. You got it. You are breathing.

The primary benefit of breathing a particular way is a fast, stress-busting remedy. Besides reducing stress, scientists have proved that intentional breathing can positively affect multiple parts of your body. Before doing my heart's walk-reset, I used deliberate breathing to help calm my fear.

The *90-Second Shift* works rapidly, moving you quickly away from struggle and fear, guiding you back to your present-moment state. Thoughtful breathing can upshift your mindset when you are in the decision-making mode.

Rather than being pushed around by the primal, reactive part of your brain known as *The Lizard Brain*, you can communicate from your heart. Subsequently, the routine of breathing a particular way can profoundly improve your health.

Remember this. Your physical body and your mind are linked, and each is affected by the other.

## THE SHIFT SEED

I was first introduced to a modified way of breathing by a respiratory therapist, who helped my husband recover from life-threatening pneumonia in 2010. With massive fluid in his lungs, Gregory's oxygen had dropped to 48%, which is devastatingly low and brain damaging.

My husband was near death and felt like he was under water. Since he has been afraid of swimming all his life, he was petrified of drowning and fed his hopelessness. He literally begged three separate nurses to euthanize him.

The respiratory therapist told Gregory to exhale through pursed lips, producing slight back pressure inside his lungs. The lungs have millions of tiny air sacs that behave like balloons. When they deflate and stick together, they require extra pressure to re-inflate, just like a balloon you once used and put away in a drawer.

When Gregory began counting in his head and exhaling through pursed lips, it looked like his mindset and body shifted in harmony. Despair left his face, and his oxygen level began to rise.

Which came first: Gregory's mindset shift or physical improvement?

His MindShift and physical change appeared simultaneous. If I had to guess, I'd wager that my husband shifted his mindset first. His mind moved away from fueling fear to counting in his head, pursing his lips, and visualizing how his lungs were filling with air.

Your mind-body connection is powerful.

Since your mind and body are interconnected, change appears to be in-sync when you fluidly shift mental gears. At the same time when gears grind, you stall and struggle.

## "90-SECOND SHIFT" OVERVIEW

Delightfully, I discovered that the easiest way to prepare for MindShifting is to consciously count during your breath cycles. Your goal is to breathe in to a number, then breathe out to double that number. Never rush. Count steadily.

Noticing the air moving in and out of your airways raises your awareness and focuses your energy. Breathing this specific way dramatically benefits your mindset and your physical body.

Counting occupies your brain and shifts your mind away from fueling negative thoughts.

When you are involved in counting, while noticing the air moving in and out of your lungs, it is virtually impossible to think about things that are worrisome.

In fact, this MindShift Exercise™ is an abbreviated process many of my coaching clients regularly use alone. The method makes a difference in their lives and for me as well.

Some people are challenged when they try to inhale to the count of 6 and exhale to 12. Make it easy on yourself and pick a breathe-in count that is comfortable for you. Add a few more counts when you exhale until you can breathe out twice as long as you inhaled.

When you attempt to exhale to the count of 12, at first it may seem to take too long. Always breathe easily without forcing it. Over time, your inhalation and exhalation will increase with practice.

Personally, I discovered that in-to-7 and out-to-14 is both invigorating and centering for me. You pick your goal numbers. They may be 5 and 10, 6 and 12, or 7 and 14. Make the process easy on yourself.

That's it. This simple manner of breathing is incredibly effective and creates fast results. So, set a simple goal and get in the flow!

## WHY IS THE "90-SECOND SHIFT" SO EFFECTIVE?

As you inhale slowly through your nose, notice your breath and silently count to yourself, so that...

- You feel the air as it flows through your nose and into your lungs.
- Your brain is focused on doing.
- Your mind shifts its perspective and moves to the present moment.
- You are aware.

As you gently exhale through pursed lips, notice your breath and silently count to yourself, so that...

- You improve your breathing process.
- You help open your lung capacity by putting slight pressure on the tiny air sacs in your lungs, similar to inflating a balloon.
- You help rid your body of carbon dioxide and increase your oxygen level.
- You sharpen your mind.

## WHAT'S THE BEST TIMING?

Add this "mighty mini" to your mental preparation ritual before, and while doing, anything. Think of this method as a reset, reboot, re-frame tool. Let me break down the concept a bit more.

Use the "90-Second Shift" BEFORE anything, such as...

- Before you start your day
- Walk into your office
- Join a business meeting
- Make a phone call
- Go on a date or attend a party
- Compete in any realm of life
- Speak in front of a group

Why? Doing a gentle reboot BEFORE you do anything releases anxiety and stress.

Include the "90-Second Shift" DURING whatever you're doing in life, such as...

- While you're at home playing with your children or grandkids
- Being a caregiver for a loved one
- Sitting at your desk or in a business meeting
- Talking on the phone
- On a date or at a party
- In an athletic competition as a professional or novice
- Giving a presentation and speaking in front of a crowd

Why? Doing a gentle reboot DURING any activity brings you back to the moment and increases your self-confidence.

Now, ask yourself, *"Where do I need the 90-Second Shift?"*

What just came to your mind? The first thought that drops into our conscious mind is our gut giving us a clue. Your unconscious mind found its voice. Write down what you heard.

## SECRET KEY

On top of everything else, I discovered an unexpected mind-body connection around breathing... *Inhaling activates certain parts of the body while exhaling settles the entire body.*

To clarify:

- **Inhaling** energizes your body while potentially releasing chemicals that trigger the "fight/flight/freeze" response to cope with perceived threats—real or imagined.

- **Exhaling** releases tension and relaxes your body, mind, and spirit.

The mind confuses the body by focusing on troubles. Stress overwhelms the body regardless of the source of the danger.

Since exhaling is the stress-buster, it became crystal clear to me that exhaling is often more effective by being twice as long as the inhale. Hence, 6 seconds in, 12 seconds out.

## JUST PRACTICE

You can take possession of this skill and make it your own by reading and doing the detailed steps that follow. When you breathe and count to yourself, there's an unexpected sweet spot that will help embed this technique and anchor it as a positive habit.

When you count in your head, focus on moving your eyes and reading each number, one after another. Once you become familiar with the process and close your eyes to step through the method, vividly "see" the numbers in your mind's eye.

**Added benefit:** By using your vision along with eye tracking muscles when counting to yourself and breathing, *you add two additional subtle body movements that further engage your body-mind connection.* The more ways you involve your body, the faster you will be able to shift your mindset.

You may think that I lean towards only doing on-the-run shifting, rather than sitting in a cross-legged pose. Please understand, taking time for yourself is vital, and meditation of any kind is valuable.

However, we spend so much time dashing around running into one road block after another, we must learn how to take a 90-second pause, release the stress, and effectively reboot.

Simply being aware of your breath is also one of the key elements of Transcendental Meditation, which has been researched for many years. In one of his articles on *Huffington Post*, Dr. Robert Schneider, one of the world's leading authorities on scientific, natural approaches for healing the body, wrote:

> *"Research on meditation has... shown a wide range of psychological benefits. [In the] 2012 review of 163 studies [that was] published by the American Psychological Association, they concluded that Transcendental Meditation had relatively strong effects in reducing anxiety [and] negative emotions... while aiding learning, memory and self-realization. Mindfulness mediation had relative strong effects in reducing negative personality traits and stress..."*

Regardless of how you breathe, do the gentle reboot *90-Second Shift* before you start anything. When you feel like you just don't have enough time, rethink that!

You can always find 90 seconds.

Let's begin.

## "90-SECOND SHIFT" DETAILED STEPS

Always breathe easily without forcing it. Make it easy on yourself and pick a breathe-in count that's comfortable for you. Add a few more counts when you exhale until you can breathe out twice as long as you inhaled.

**Step 1: Close your eyes, sit comfortably, and prepare to shift.** Relax your shoulders. Begin to notice the air as you breathe.

**Step 2: Take three slow, deep breaths.** Inhale and exhale as you silently count to yourself. Inhale through your nose to the count of 6, exhale through pursed lips to the count of 12. As you consciously breathe, visualize and follow the number with your eyes, noticing the air as it travels its course. Breathe slowly, counting as far as you can, like this:

> **Breath #1:**
>
> Inhale through your nose... *one, two, three, four, five, six*
>
> Exhale through pursed lips... *one, two, three, four, five, six, seven, eight, nine, ten, eleven, twelve*

**Breath #2:** Repeat breathing in and out as you count silently to yourself and follow the numbers as above.

**Breath #3:** Repeat breathing in and out as you count.

**Step 3: Smile.** Feel the smile light up your face. Even if you are seated in a dimly lit room, envision the warmth of the sun on your face.

## BONUS TIP

Consider using the *90-Second Shift* when you can't get to sleep at night.

Your mind may be keeping you awake by jumping from one thought to another, focusing on what went wrong, or continually revising your must-do list. This simple process can effectively remove you from the state of sleeplessness, allowing your mind and body to relax and fall asleep.

## VALIDATION

Breathing is a balancing and energizing tool. For my personal self-care and to expand my knowledge, I became a certified QiGong Instructor in 2015. QiGong is pronounced "chee-gong" and is an ancient Chinese healthcare system that is over 5,000 years old.

When I went to a national convention earlier that year, I was delighted to discover a wonderful similarity between the QiGong philosophy and what I do:

**QiGong** integrates physical postures, breathing techniques and focused intentions.

**MindShift Exercises**™ intentionally use subtle body movements to engage your body-mind connection, which is amplified by conscious breathing.

Going through the testing process to become a certified instructor clearly reinforced that what I am doing is exactly where I am supposed to be. I have now become a hybrid: *Eastern Medicine Philosopher coupled with Western Medicine Advocate.*

Along with having regular physicals and creating a strong communication bond with our doctors, I believe we must take a more active role in our health.

By adopting healthier behaviors, we can manage our own stress and transform our lifestyle. By integrating MindShifting into your daily life, you might just stay ahead of the curve and live a longer, more rewarding life.

**Want a memory jogger?** If so, plan on writing or printing "flash cards" for the QuickShift™ versions of each MindShift Exercise™. It's my intention to help you recall how to do a MindShift with simple reminders. For the *90-Second Shift*, use in-and-out counts that are most comfortable for you. Set your goal to exhale to a count that's twice as long as you inhale.

### "90-SECOND SHIFT" QUICKSHIFT™

1. **Get comfortable.** Close your eyes, sit comfortably, and relax your shoulders.

2. **Notice the air moving as you breathe: In to 6, out to 12.** Count in your mind and "see" the numbers. As you inhale through your nose, count to 6. As you slowly exhale through softly, pursed lips, count to 12.

3. **Smile when you finish.** Notice how much better you feel.

### PROGRESS CONFIRMATION

Since you've experienced your third MindShift Exercise™ *90-Second Shift*, it's time to say the following aloud:

> *"Now that I have learned how to gently reboot with the 90-Second Shift, I am taking control of my mind and my body."*

### UP NEXT...

In the next chapter, I'll show you how to become aware *the instant* your energy begins to shift in a dangerous direction. You will discover how negative energy around you can dramatically affect you.

Your upcoming MindShift Exercise™ is called *Engage Your Energetic Radar,* and it will become your *Energetic Vaccine* to counteract *Energetic Flu.*

The method gives you added protection while reinforcing your natural immune system by raising your awareness. When we are unaware, our energy fields can become infected.

Let's face it. We all need an *Energetic Vaccination.*

# CHAPTER 7
# ENERGETIC RADAR (MSE 4)

In this chapter, you'll learn your fourth MindShift Exercise™, *Engage Your Energetic Radar.*

This method raises your awareness as your energy shifts. You receive alerts when your energy changes, much like setting an automatic "internal alarm clock."

When you are genuinely alerted while your energy shifts towards negativity, the process of knowing is empowering. Plus, the awareness puts you back in control.

## WHERE'S THE INFECTION?

External dark energy infects our energy field when we absorb the negativity and hold onto misery.

To make matters worse, we self-infect when we continually focus on our flaws, our mistakes, and our woe-is-me drama.

*Infected energy field? Seriously?*

Yes. As odd as it sounds, we catch *Energetic Flu* from the sludge around us and from heartless self-judgment. Sadly, the *Energetic Flu season* is year round. The bug is everywhere and is highly contagious.

We definitely need an *Energetic Vaccine.*

## ENERGETIC FLU UNDER A MICROSCOPE

When you are unaware, you are a puppet. You become a slave to both your internal energy and to all the muck that surrounds you. You are clearly not a septic tank, but you unconsciously hold onto garbage.

Even though you're convinced you're doing your best, when unmindful, you're out of balance and your actions tilt. You are out of control.

With no apparent reason, you raise your voice. You become angry. You speed up and eventually crash.

For years, self-deprecating thoughts dropped into my mind out of the blue. I was confused. Where did the thoughts come from? I didn't understand how they controlled me, but they did.

Looking back, I now see a giant invisible finger moving me around like an icon on the touchscreen of a smartphone or computer tablet. I heard a deep, hellish, commanding voice yelling, *"Here? There? NO! INTO THE TRASH."*

I eventually discovered that my behavior was affected by more than just my own thoughts. External energy seemed to literally alter my mindset.

Finally, I realized my state of mind and my thoughts were reactive. Both my mindset and my thoughts were victims of negative energetic intrusion. I was continually in one unconscious "do-loop" after another.

## EVERYTHING IS ENERGY

Our mindset is affected by energy. Everything around us—other people, places, things, ideas, and sounds—has electromagnetic energy fields that impact our minds. Energetically, *everything* can affect and alter our mindset.

The key to being in command of our own mindset is twofold:

- Recognize when our energy shifts from positive to negative.
- Then, consciously take appropriate action.

Controlling our mind is that simple and clear cut: Become aware of the darkness, then intentionally act rather than automatically react.

Sometimes, you might physically feel a colossal hand coming out of a black cloud, attempting to seize you. I have had that experience. When I was unaware, the power of darkness eclipsed me. I was frustrated, anxious, and weakened.

Once I realized that I needed a system to alert me as my own energy shifted, I finally figured out what to do.

## WHAT IS ENERGETIC RADAR?

My coaching clients kept asking, *"What exactly do you mean by energetic radar?"*

I believed it was enough to say, "Just be aware and shift," but I was mistaken. They wanted detailed explanations. They needed to know exactly how to sense when their energy shifted to negativity. Otherwise, they became overwhelmed.

It has taken a long time to verbalize what I've been doing for decades. I guess I was the incubator, where I was infected by negative energy. Within myself, I created an *Energetic Vaccine*, which fortified my natural immune system.

There's nothing mystical or magical about energetic defenses. They are real and have existed all along. It's not rocket science, but it has taken me what seems like forever to put this thought-concept into words.

## BETTER THAN NEEDLES

Simply acknowledge the existence of your energetic defense system. Then, launch your defenses by activating and engaging, which is all that is required of you.

Instead of giving yourself an *Energetic Flu shot*, consider cultivating your customized *Energetic Vaccine* inside your mind in the form of an *Energetic Radar*. Uniquely yours. Defined and created by you, for you.

Let me set the stage...

Think about the numerous ways Highway Patrol measures your car's energy, or its speed: radar, hand-held laser device, pacing with an aircraft, and tracking speed with their vehicle. The radar gun is the top choice of many cops.

When a patrolman discovers you are speeding, they sound their siren, flash their lights, and pull you over. You put on your brakes. Your energy is affected by what happens around you. *"Dang it. Caught again!"*

A radar speed gun is used to measure energy in sports and races, such as the speed of a pitched baseball, a runner, a tennis serve, a racing horse, a greyhound dog, or even a golf ball.

Consider this: Whenever we are unaware while driving a vehicle, our speed often increases. Speed creeps up, a little at a time. In a brief moment, we might be way over the speed limit and in danger. We clearly need an *Energetic Cruise Control.*

Negative energy shifts happen in all areas of our life, just like driving. The perfect solution for measuring the shift in your energy is using your own *Energetic Radar.*

The method will help you create your radar system by imagining it. Here's an example.

## CASE STUDY

Late one evening, one of my coaching clients sent a text asking for a private, early-morning session. I knew she'd been dealing with stress and harassment at her job for a long time. As a result, I suspected she was finally seeking alternate employment.

From my point of view, it appeared that it was way past her time to let go. In life, sometimes we keep holding onto a losing situation because it's too hard for us to loosen our grip. We just don't want to give up in a relationship, at work, or even in our thoughts. We feel like we're a failure if we let go and move on.

My text back to my client, "What do you want to do?"

Her text reply, "I want to find a place of calm and peace before I enter an important meeting."

I sent her the call-in numbers for our 8:15 AM meeting and set my alarm for 6:00 AM. That was early for me.

Despite the fact that I'm a natural early riser, I've moved my biological clock to accommodate both my personal lifestyle and after-hours coaching. Oftentimes, people need to be off-the-clock and away from their day job in order to focus on themselves, whether they are executives, business owners, or worker bees.

In the morning, we met on our private conference line. My client's words were halting and they surprised me. Even though she's a strong, empowered woman, her voice was weak and frail. Her mindset was fractured. She was gripped by fear.

"How may I help you this morning?" I asked.

Unexpectedly, her energy had shifted and was weakened. Her words that follow LOOK self-confident, however, they came from the voice of a meek, little girl.

She replied, "In ninety minutes, I'll be in a meeting regarding harassment at my work place. I want to ensure I'm in the best state of mind. I want to ensure I am in a confident mindset, that words come to me easily, and I am communicating effectively."

She had to step back into her power. It became apparent that she was attached to the outcome. She was frozen, like prey backed into a corner by a predator.

## PREPARE TO ENGAGE

Our mindset-shifting "muscles" are just like any other muscle in our body—unless we exercise them, they wither and die.

You may be unaware that mindset-mental muscles exist. Be patient. They do exist, and they will surface as we go along. Flexing your mental muscles revives them.

Each time you do an exercise, you'll discover it has a life of its own. As you add a mental exercise to your toolbox, the technique naturally transforms.

Your life experience and your personal energy can transform each MindShift Exercise™ and become singularly yours. Each exercise mirrors you and helps you learn about your own energy.

Since my client's energy was fragmented before her job harassment case meeting, we started with the *90-Second Shift*—the fast-acting method to balance and center oneself that I shared with you in the previous chapter. Then, I helped her fashion and engage her own *Energetic Radar*.

Let's discover your *Energetic Radar* now.

## "ENERGETIC RADAR" DETAILED STEPS

By following along while I guide you through this 9-step process, you can identify and activate your *Energetic Radar*.

At first, the process may seem abstract, but stay with me. Going through the process is interesting and fun. Frankly, you may benefit more than you expect.

### Step 1: Close your eyes. Mentally move outside your body.

In your mind's eye, see yourself standing directly in front of you. Your feet are shoulder-width apart and you are standing firmly on the ground.

Stand barefooted and connect with Mother Earth. Visualize cords going from your feet, deep into the center of the earth, and plugged into Mother Earth's energy field.

If you're tense, your shoulders will be raised up close to your ears. Physically and gently move your shoulders down and back. Stretch.

Inhale deeply. Exhale slowly as you drop your shoulders and relax. Smile.

### Step 2: Place your hands on your hips. Feel your power.

As you stand there with your feet apart, physically place your hands on your hips at your waist and feel your power. See yourself standing in your power with your head held high.

Slowly breathe in and out. See, feel, and savor your unique awesomeness.

### Step 3: Mentally move back inside your body. Look down.

Keep your eyes closed. In your mind's eye, switch from looking at yourself, to being inside of you, looking outward. *Whoosh!*

Looking out through your own eyes, look down around your body and notice the shining energy field surrounding you. Your energy radiates like the sun and glows all around your body.

### Step 4: Meet your Energetic Radar and get acquainted.

Look down. You're wearing a pleasing belt around your waist. On your belt is an apparatus that controls your *Energetic Radar.* You can call it whatever you like, such as: the *Controller, Chief, Master,* or *Boss.*

Mine is the *Governor,* which is a speed limiter or device that measures and regulates the speed of an engine, just like a cruise control. You pick your title. From here on, I'll refer to it as *Governor* or *device.*

Reach down with your hand, and take the device off your belt. Concentrate on the gadget you're holding and smile. Immediately, feel your gratitude.

Think about how quickly your *Energetic Radar* notices the changes in your energy field and alerts you:

- The moment a negative thought drops into your mind
- When you're physically in a negative space
- When you're energetically at risk

What does your *Governor* look like?

Ask your *Energetic Radar Governor* to take form. Hold it in both hands, breathe deeply, and smile. Caress it. Inspect it. Discover its mass. Feel how substantial it is.

The *Governor* morphs into any form or shape you would like it to be. See it changing in front of your eyes right now, feeling it with your hands.

Mine originally looked like a hair dryer. Then, it changed and transformed as it became part of me.

A client reported: "My Energetic Radar took the form of a bright light saber and I named it the *Energetic Radar Saber.*"

Take a moment right now and decide what your *Energetic Radar Governor* looks like. See it and describe it to yourself.

**Step 5: Activate, then "pair and connect" your Energetic Radar.**

Look down at the base of your radar's *Governor* and find a toggle switch. There is a red "OFF" below the switch. Right now, the switch is in the off-position.

Above the switch, there is a green "ON." Reach down and flip the switch to the on-position.

You have activated your *Energetic Radar.*

Now, you are in the setup/configuration mode where you energetically "pair" with your radar, just like connecting your smartphone to a wireless device. Hold the *Governor* close to your heart and gently tap your chest several times. You are pairing.

Breathe in deeply. Sense your connection. Enjoy the feeling, while slowly exhaling.

Your entire body is now paired with your *Energetic Radar Governor.* Smile.

**Step 6: Notice the scope of your *Energetic Radar*.**

Rather than using your radar in a single, pinpoint direction like a standard radar gun, your *Energetic Radar* scans a 360-degree field around you. Besides warning you when you slip into a personal negative space, it also alerts you when negativity surrounds you.

You always have the choice to either disengage from external negativity or buy into that negative energy. You have the choice. When you're aware, you can protect and shield yourself.

As your *Energetic Radar* probes the 360 degrees around you, it engages more than just a circle. It functions in a total sphere. You are safely nestled inside your protective radar bubble.

Your *Energetic Radar* serves two purposes: It alerts you to negative energy, and reinforces your *Energetic Egg*, which protects you. (You will find *The Egg* in a later chapter.)

**Step 7: Watch as your *Energetic Radar Governor* shrinks and becomes weightless.**

As you hold your *Energetic Radar Governor* in your hand, watch it literally shrink. Allow it to become smaller and smaller.

Although the size continues to shrink, full power remains on. The system is ultra-high tech, storing a massive amount of data in a tiny space.

The *Governor* becomes smaller and smaller, until it is featherweight. In fact, it is now weightless. Your *Energetic Radar* is still on and fully powered at 100%. You are paired and engaged. Only you can see the *Governor*, which weighs absolutely nothing.

**Step 8: Install your *Energetic Radar Governor* permanently in a discrete location on your body.**

Decide where you're going to wear your *Energetic Radar Governor* on your body. (Yes, even though it is invisible to the physical eye, your *Energetic Radar* can remain with you indefinitely.)

You can wear it as a ring, on a bracelet, a necklace, around your ankle, or on a belt. You can envision your radar as a tattoo, let the device sit on your shoulder, or even merge it with your skin. Wherever you want your *Energetic Radar* to reside, simply install it there.

Now softly tap that location five times. By tapping, you are stimulating your body-mind connection with subtle body movements. If for some reason, you are unable to physically tap, or you prefer to remain perfectly still, mentally tap.

If you decide to move the location of your radar later, that's perfectly okay. You can move it and reinstall, by consciously tapping the new location five times.

You have now engaged your *Energetic Radar*.

**Step 9: Forgive yourself and take action.**

Remember, the intended purpose of your *Energetic Radar* is to alert you when...

- A negative thought creeps into your mind
- You continue to think negatively
- Negativity is around you or enters your energy field

When alerted by your *Energetic Radar*, you become awake. At the moment you awaken, forgive yourself for being asleep at the wheel and shift into a positive gear.

Your *Energetic Radar* is now installed, activated, and paired.

## "ENERGETIC RADAR" AT-A-GLANCE

1. **Close your eyes. Mentally move outside your body.** See yourself standing directly in front of you, barefooted and plugged into Mother Earth's energy field.

2. **Place your hands on your hips and stand in your power.** Breathe. See, feel, and savor your power.

3. **Mentally move back inside your body.** Look down at your body and notice the shining energy field surrounding you.

4. **Meet your *Energetic Radar Governor* and get acquainted.** Describe the controller to yourself, calling your device whatever you like.

5. **Activate your *Energetic Radar*.** Flip the switch to the ON position, tap to pair and connect.

6. **Notice the scope of your *Energetic Radar*, which functions in a total sphere around you.** You are nestled inside your protective radar bubble as your *Energetic Radar* scans a 360-degree field in all directions around you.

7. **Watch as your *Energetic Radar Governor* shrinks and becomes weightless.** Your *Energetic Radar* is still on and fully powered at 100%.

8. **Permanently install your *Energetic Radar Governor* in a discrete location of your choosing.** To install, softly tap on that location five times.

9. **Forgive yourself and take action.** When you are alerted by your *Energetic Radar*, you become awake. At the moment you awaken, forgive yourself for being asleep at the wheel and shift into a positive gear.

## YOUR "ENERGETIC RADAR" CAN SHORT CIRCUIT

Even though you have engaged and permanently installed your *Energetic Radar*, something odd can happen: If you receive no alerts when negativity affects you, your radar might have blown a circuit.

When we're in emotional turmoil, we often experience power surges.

Think of having an electrical surge in the kitchen. Usually a ground fault outlet interrupts the electrical power. Generally in your home, all you have to do is depress the reset button on the outlet, and electricity flows once again.

To reconfigure your *Energetic Radar Governor,* tap five times on the location where you originally installed your radar. Take a few minutes and go through your initial steps to re-engage.

If you prefer, move the location and start over. This time the *Install-Activate-Pair* process will be a quick install.

**Want an almost instant re-install?** Sometimes I feel like my *Energetic Radar* signal is missing in action. I seem to be stuck on an emotional roller coaster.

Where did my radar go? I want my automatic, internal alert system back. I want to re-install right now!

You might experience the same thing. If so, don't despair. Your *Energetic Radar* is right there within you.

Let's compare re-install to what might happen when you lose your phone's connection during a call.

> **Scenario 1:** You're talking on your cell phone and your phone instantly loses its signal without notice. You talk and talk, getting no response. There's no one on the line

but you. You attempt to call back, but your signal won't go through. You redial and redial and redial to no avail. You're frustrated.

**Scenario 2:** You're on the line with an important person who is saying something you need to hear. There is static and interference on the phone line, and you say, "I'll call you right back." You hang up and immediately call back. The connection is perfectly clear. You're delighted.

Pick Scenario 2 as your mental framework for the QuickShift™ below and revel in the fact that you can reconnect swiftly.

Hopefully by now, you've fully grasped the concept of your *Energetic Radar* by going through the 9-step process.

For me, the following QuickShift™ is a simple reminder. Periodically, I step through the process, which has become a comforting experience.

With a little bit of practice, you might experience the same feeling.

### "ENERGETIC RADAR" QUICKSHIFT™

1. **Close your eyes. Breathe deeply as you lovingly hold your *Energetic Radar Governor* in your hands.** Flip the switch to OFF, then back to ON, just as you would with an electric circuit breaker.

2. **Tap five times on any preferred spot on your body.** You've now installed, activated, and paired your *Energetic Radar* with your mind.

3. **Forgive yourself when your *Energetic Radar* alerts you that you're asleep at the wheel.** Upshift. Detach and observe. Decide your best action with the information you have, and take action.

## PROGRESS CONFIRMATION

Since you have now experienced your fourth MindShift Exercise™ *Energetic Radar,* you are indeed protecting yourself. Intentionally say the following aloud:

> *"I am taking control of my mind and creating an uplifted life, now that I have installed and engaged my Energetic Radar to alert me when internal energy shifts in the wrong direction."*

## UP NEXT...

In Chapter 8, you'll find the approach I discovered more than thirty years ago to stop sabotaging myself. The method morphed into a loving, gentle way to trigger a MindShift within myself and with those near me. My husband and I still use the process today, and I continually use it with my coaching clients.

The upcoming MindShift Exercise™ called *Tag,* is an upgrade "plugin" for your *Energetic Radar.* What a novel concept!

Be sure to read on and install your Energetic Radar plugin, *Tag.*

# Chapter 8
# Tag (MSE 5)

In this chapter, your fifth MindShift Exercise™ is *Tag*. This method is a loving, gentle way to trigger a positive MindShift by changing your words. My belief is this: *"The words you choose set yourself up for either success or failure."*

Over the years, I realized that every self-defeating word is a ticking time bomb. *Tick... Tick... Tick...*

Unfortunately, we rarely examine our word choice by listening to the words as they come out of our mouth. We virtually never even consider if our words are positive or negative before we speak.

For your convenience, *Tag* is now your *Energetic Radar "Plugin"* that will help widen your radar's field.

## WHAT WORDS TELL YOU

Your words are a reflection of your thoughts. Your thoughts are a direct result of your beliefs. It follows, since your words are clues to what you're thinking, they reveal what you believe. Your words are your mindset mirror and a creation tool.

When we consciously change the words that come out of our mouth, we transform our mindset. Words, thoughts, and beliefs live together in your mind. They nurture and feed each other to produce both our positive and negative perceptions. Therefore, consider this:

- Your beliefs generate your thoughts.
- Your thoughts craft your words.
- Your words create your reality.

The relationship of the belief-thought-word trio fashions your life. They collaborate. Their interaction, or synergy, is the foundation of your life, built block by block.

Underneath the thought-word stream, consider the *echo back* of your thoughts. Imagine a rubber ball bouncing back from a wall. That's what happens in a micro second when you first have a thought. You send a thought out to the universe; it bounces back and gets stronger.

Even though many people believe their life is cemented in rock and permanent, it is not. Rather than being cut in stone, we can change our life fluidly by changing the words we speak.

*Could life be that simple?*

## DISCOVERING THE POWER OF WORDS

I first realized the power of words during a weeklong training in the mid '80s in Orlando, Florida. The workshop was about Neuro-Linguistic Programming or NLP.

Throughout that week, I sowed seeds that began to re-form my limiting beliefs. As I awakened, my thoughts and existence began to change and multiply like growing corn.

When a farmer grows corn, the seedlings are fragile as they first peek out of the ground. In only a day or two, the corn gains strength and stands erect. In 60 days, one stalk of corn grows from a single kernel and usually produces 2 ears of corn with an average of 800 kernels each. One kernel can produce up to 1,600 seeds!

*Always be aware of the seeds you sow.*

The deliberate process that I learned during the NLP training continues to improve my life today. I will openly share how it works and explain its simplicity to you in this chapter. My family and friends benefit greatly because I am now a lot more pleasant to be around.

The system was cutting-edge back then. Now I believe it continues to be just as groundbreaking today. Frankly, I think the significance of the training is often overlooked because its label is odd and confusing. Neuro-Linguistic Programming, or NLP, still makes me furrow my brow and squint my eyes when someone says it quickly, or when I see it in print.

When you hear anything that confuses you, it leaves you wondering. A confused mind rarely accepts a concept or purchases a product. One of the primary rules in advertising and marketing is, "A confused mind never buys."

When you see confusion on someone's face, it gives you a clue that something is muddled. They may be stuck in their belief-thought-act loop.

## UNSPOKEN WORDS

That reminds me of the significance of seeing fleeting changes, or *micro-expressions*, on a person's face. They give us clues about that person's mindset. The slightest facial muscle twitch might tell us that concealed emotions are being rapidly processed. I often think of this type of twitch as an "emotional flash."

These emotion-based expressions occur so fast that most people cannot see or recognize them in real time. We may be unsure what an elusive expression means. However, it may possibly be one of six things:

1. The person likes what just happened.

2. They dislike what just happened.

3. They are confused by their situation.

4. They are trying to conceal their emotions.

5. It is an involuntary tick.

6. It means nothing at all.

The first time we see a person's facial-flash, we rarely know what that means. However, the flashes hint at what's going on inside that person. Before we can pinpoint the meaning of a subtle expression, we might need to see it multiple times.

We also need to understand the decisions he or she might be considering. Then, we can formulate an assumption and start creating a profile. By observing actions and spoken words of others, we are given insight into their thoughts and feelings, clearly illustrating the connection between physical actions and words.

We can also see the same connection in ourselves. Our thoughts become words and actions. Those words and actions reinforce how we feel or believe about what's going on.

## EXAMPLE OF UNSPOKEN WORD SIGNALS

While I was writing this book, people's visual reaction to the working cover design gave me clear feedback about what worked and what did not. The original draft cover was a graphic of a red, manual gearshift knob, which I loved. It became difficult for me to let it go until I got the message.

To avoid mixed signals from multiple people, I made it a point to show the cover to one person at a time from my phone's screen. Without a doubt, every response told me the graphics and layout were vibrant, but the visuals failed to pair with the words. I clearly missed the point.

Virtually everyone's face lit up when they saw the gearshift; however, while reading the lengthy working title, they paused and remained silent. Many flashed a rapid eye squint and furrowed their brow.

The way their faces changed told me the words puzzled them. I needed to say more with less. Yet, their faces gave me another, non-verbal message I kept missing.

My Takeaway: I had another forehead-smack moment. Yes, the gearshift graphic was clever, but visually the shift knob sent the wrong message, triggering unintended thoughts that sent the reader down a rabbit hole.

The working cover looked like the book had something to do with cars, or maybe racing, completely missing the fact that I was sharing ways to shift your mental gears inside your head.

*Duh! Smack!* Sometimes ego sidetracks and lures you away from the highest good. Mine did.

## FROGS INTO PRINCES

The Neuro-Linguistic Programming workshop, which introduced me to the power of words, was based on the book *Frogs into Princes.* The publication was an edited transcript of a live training done in 1979 by the founders of NLP, Richard Bandler and John Grinder.

Simply put, NLP focuses on better communication skills, but not in the way you might think. Instead of being just about talking with others, it goes to the source, talking to your SELF first. That's why I use the phrase *"the words you speak."*

*Rather than positive thinking, it's about precise thinking.* The more exact you make your thinking, the more clearly and accurately you will be understood.

Think about the last time you had a bad day. It may have seemed as if one crappy thing happened after another.

Chances are you were talking to yourself in counterproductive terms. You were asking yourself questions like, "Why can't I...?" or "Why do I always...?"

First, this type of word selection creates a negative focus for your mind. Second, your words give your unconscious mind harmful and often destructive questions to answer.

> *Asking self "Why do I always screw up?" gives your subconscious mind the programming language it uses to produce more dangerous results.*

That's GIGO in action—Garbage In, Garbage Out. In computer science terms, GIGO is defined this way: "Computers will unquestioningly process unintended input and produce undesired output."

That's exactly what happens to people. *That is precisely how our subconscious mind works.*

Our subconscious is a perfect computer. It records everything without questioning its validity. That's garbage in.

However, the garbage-out mechanism is flawed. If it weren't so ugly, I'd call it elegant.

Our subconscious is a lousy playback system. It selectively replays emotionally charged information. What we put in with highly-charged emotion comes out quicker and louder. That's a simple description of Post-Traumatic Stress Disorder (PTSD).

After a person experiences a terrifying event, or ordeal, filled with emotions or grave physical harm, that situation is deep seated in their subconscious. They often re-live the experience in nightmares or flashbacks. The traumas keep popping up in their conscious mind without warning.

When you continually say harmful words to yourself during a bad day, those words are magnified by damaging, emotional feelings. You get more of the same.

*A field of fertilized negativity yields a hardy crop of hopelessness.*

## HOW TO STOP "GARBAGE IN"

When I returned home from that NLP weeklong workshop, I knew I *must become aware of my words in order to control my mindset.* I also wanted to change my words in a forgiving way.

How could I *interrupt* my thought-words without judging? If I blamed myself for thinking the words, that would only create reaction and more of the same.

What could I do once the words came out of my mouth? When I spoke negatively, were the words permanent?

When I said condescending words to myself, was I destined to create more garbage? Or could I take those words back, like a commander ordering troops to fall back, retreat and regroup?

Yes, I could change my words! However, I realized I had to design a method that was both loving and forgiving, one without judgment.

## THE RESULT

To successfully shift both my thought-words and spoken-words, I made a casual request to self, *"Find other words to say the same thing."* These few words became a *pattern interrupt.*

The request gave instructions to my mind to change my words, which opened the door to shift negative words to positive ones without blame. There are five simple steps to trigger changing your words in an easy-breezy way.

- Breathe
- Smile
- Tone
- Time
- Awareness

## "TAG" DETAILED STEPS

While this 5-step method is an easy way to re-train your mind, it is precise, going far deeper than *"the words you say."* The method engages other senses to speed-shift the results.

**Step 1: Breathe.** This may sound oversimplified to you. However, when you consciously take a deep breath, you shift to neutral and move to the moment.

Mindfully pause. Slowly breathe in and out before starting to speak. In a few seconds, you have the time to settle and collect your thoughts.

A single breath becomes a forgiving, decision-making way of changing your words. When you knowingly breathe before you speak, you shift your mental gears.

**Step 2: Smile and drop your shoulders.** Both actions relieve stress. Physically smiling can change your perception of what is happening. A frown overshadows your words, even when you intend to forgive yourself for what you just said.

By dropping your shoulders as you smile, you let go of punishing yourself for saying particular words.

**Step 3: Your tone is important.** Whether I said to myself silently or out loud, *"Find other words to say the same thing,"* my tone and word selection mattered and made a big difference.

Said one way, the phrase sounds like an authoritative order, which produces a reaction within. Imagine a drill sergeant shouting, *"Find other words to say the same thing... Re-phrase!"* I bet you heard that in your head and felt a reaction.

Said another way, it's a loving, accepting request. Acceptance allows you to work through the process internally (without guilt) while you select healthier words.

Visualize a nurturing mother gently hugging her baby and cooing, *"Find other words to say the same thing... Re-phrase."* I suspect you heard that in your head, and a smile came over your face.

Right now, say the re-set phrase aloud both ways and see which feels better. It's a fact that smiling or frowning affects our body's chemistry. One builds and nurtures, while the other disrupts and damages our frame of mind.

- **Be bossy.** State your command with a frown on your face: *"Find other words to say the same thing... Re-phrase!"*
- **Be loving and forgiving.** Make your request with a twinkle in your eye and a smile on your face: "Find other words to say the same thing... Re-phrase."

**Step 4: It takes time.** It took more time than I expected to learn how to reconstruct a phrase so that the words no longer crippled me. Often, when I interrupted my self-talk, it took a while to come up with a positive solution. That's okay.

Replace all negative words. Be sure to always, *always*, ALWAYS keep *NOT* and *DON'T* out of your language. Please forgive me when I use them when I write.

If you tell a child, "Don't touch the burners on top of the stove," guess what happens? They reach out to touch the scalding hot burners.

Even if you lovingly tell your partner, "Please don't do xyz," guess what? They probably do just that since their subconscious heard, "Please do xyz."

Your subconscious *auto-eliminates* the words NOT and DON'T. It literally takes the words out of the sentence.

Granted, it takes practice and patience to locate correct words. The process will pay off in real time by up-shifting both your subconscious mind and your life.

**Step 5: It requires staying aware.** For me, discovering awareness was both perplexing and challenging. The habit of thinking negative thoughts had become automatic and was a part of my mere existence. When thoughts hopped around in my mind, out-of-control words spewed out my mouth.

When my *Energetic Radar* alerted me that what I had just said was downshifting, all I needed was to respond forgivingly. In reality, once you install your own *Energetic Radar*, it simply moves your mind to awareness and tells you something is amiss, just like a radar gun flagging your speed. Once you are aware, it is easy to repair.

## PLEASE RE-PHRASE

A few months after developing this method of changing my spoken words, I met my husband, Gregory. Both of us agreed to make the same request when we heard damaging words come out of the other's mouth.

To insure it remained a loving request, we added "please" at the beginning:

> *"Please, find other words to say the same thing. Please re-phrase."*

Before requesting, the habit of slowly breathing in and out shifted our mental gears. We became aware, conscious of our words, tone, and timing. It helped us build a strong foundation for our lives together.

We gently used the pattern interrupt with agents in our real estate office, both when we debriefed our own sales call, and in our personal life. Over time, Gregory and I created a one word cue that replaced, *"Please re-phrase."* It became *"Tag"* and remains the word we still use today.

*Tagging* in a loving, forgiving way continues to improve our relationship, eliminates stress and interrupts self-sabotage. The custom naturally transitioned to being an essential part of working with clients today.

## TAGGING SHIFTS MINDSET

Yes, I admit it. From time to time, unwelcome words still tumble out of my mouth. Thankfully, they are rare. However, they are a blessing.

Negative words are a heads-up that my mind has taken a detour. That way I can shift my words before an undesirable thought takes root.

During group coaching as one individual at a time takes the *safe seat,* I do a bit of housekeeping. Regardless of the industry, from entry level to the highest-level of executives, I start the same way:

- *"Be aware of the words that come out of your mouth. Notice them."*
- *"Do I have permission to Tag you?"*

During coaching, I use *Tag* for more than its original purpose of recognizing self-defeating words and shifting them. It's a gentle *pattern interrupt* intended to bring my coaching clients back to center and to the sound of my voice.

When I started privately coaching my clients in the midst of situations that were critical to them, I experienced a big shift. I discovered using *Tag* was a powerful tool to effectively coach in real time.

My clients needed to change their words and shift their mindset instantly. Otherwise, their mind remained their worst enemy.

When a client calls me during a short break, they rush and start speed-talking. They instantly focus on what had gone wrong, their mistakes, how poorly they made decisions, and how unlucky they had been.

When a person goes on and on about one mistake after another, they create more of the same. Their words are a reflection of their beliefs, mindset and actions.

They believe they are attracting bad situations. When they make poor decisions and expect they will fail, they do.

It happens in all areas of life. People continually shoot themselves in the foot, and I hear them do it every single day.

## CASE STUDY

A friend, who is a top-notch professional speaker, sent me an email with the unexpected subject line, "another little resource." When I opened the email, there were two words that jumped out at me, "little" and "try." My friend's email went like this.

> *I created a one-page sheet with the top twenty people I hire online where they will start working for as little as $5. I've been asked over and over, who are the great people I use. So I will try selling that list tonight for $20. I've attached it for you as a little resource. Hope it helps you!*

My response:

> *First, let me thank you for sharing your priceless resource. Okay, here goes. I'll be your coach for a moment. This is what I call Tag, not in terms of social media or the Internet, but like the child's game.*

> *It's a gentle nudge to shift your mindset when you use two words that work against you: try & little.*

> *'Try'*

> *You said, "So I will try selling that list tonight for $20."*

More than sixty years ago, my Mother helped shift my mindset by saying, "Stop trying... that's too much like crying. Just do it."

Rather than "try to sell" it, please, re-phrase and find other words to say the same thing, such as:

- I offer this business resource for only $20.
- For only $20, it's a gift that will save you a tremendous amount of time!
- It is a giveaway at $20 and worth three times that small investment.

How long did it take you to sift through the mass of people and come up with this list?

This is golden! This is THE solution to my frustrations with outsourcing and my hesitations when considering working with any outsourcing site.

Suggested assignment: Right now, please shift your mindset about the value of this resource, and honor the time it took you to glean and sift through the chaff.

Take a moment to send love and energy to your one-page resource. See it becoming huge and growing. Imbue it with productivity and ease so that anyone using it is energized and in the flow, effortlessly moving toward the successful completion of their goals.

Okay. That last paragraph in my email response sounds a lot like the child's dancing game Hokey-Pokey. "Turn yourself around. Put your left foot in. Put your left foot out."

Yes, simply visualizing you are sending love and energy to anything infuses that thing with positive vibrations. You know haters do exactly the opposite.

Let's go on to the second word and more of the email back to my friend.

'Little'

When you wrote "a little resource," my response was, "Little, my butt! It is not a little resource." Rather, it is condensed for the busy professional. Your resource is a concentrated serum that cures the dreaded disease of overwhelm.

Hmm, that sounds good to me.

Rather than tell yourself, it's "just a little resource," please, find other words to say the same thing, such as:

- This dynamic resource gives you twenty people who produce great results!
- It is an executive summary with twenty top producers, rather than long pages to flip through.
- At a glance, you can quickly select from twenty professionals.

After my email reply to my friend, she took immediate action. She changed her words, which produced dramatic results. She looked at what she had put together in a much different way. Instead of apologizing for creating a one-sheet list, she embraced its value and was proud of her own actions.

Rather than reluctance from her audience, they were excited. Over 50% of a huge room full of attendees ran up holding a $20 bill in their hands and picked up the executive summary!

## THE SIMPLE WORD CHANGE

Even though I came across this concept of "changing the words you say" when I attended the NLP seminar in the '80s, my mother had literally done the same thing when I was a child. She changed words in the famous children's book, *The Little Engine That Could*. Written in 1930, the book focused on the value of optimism.

As the small, locomotive engine struggles to pull a huge load up a steep mountain, it continually said, *"I think I can. I think I can."*

Once the engine inched over the top of the mountain, it shouted out, *"I knew I could! I knew I could!"* In one version, as the engine crested the peak, it shouted, *"I thought I could!"*

Reading the book to me, Mother instantly changed, *"I think I can,"* to, *"I know I can,"* as the engine neared the top of the sheer incline. By changing the words, she vividly imprinted *"I know I can"* on my mind. I believed I could accomplish whatever I wanted, then, and still believe that today. For that, I am forever grateful to my mother.

## "TAG" AT-A-GLANCE

1. **Breathe.** When you realize a negative word just came out of your mouth, consciously take a slow, deep breath and shift to neutral.

2. **Smile and drop your shoulders.** Physically smile with your face muscles, your eyes, your mouth and gently drop your shoulders.

3. **Soften your tone.** Be forgiving as you give yourself loving directions, *"Please find other words to say the same thing,"* or simply say, *"Tag."*

4. **Take your time.** Take as much times as you wish to restructure what you said so the words no longer sabotage you.

5. **Be aware.** Remain aware of the words that come into your mind and out your mouth.

**Remember:** *Tag* is your *Energetic Radar "Plugin"*. In your mind's eye, see *Tag* imprinted on your *Energetic Radar* device, or on a small piece of hardware, like a flash drive or tiny dongle, that is physically plugged into the radar's port. You are now aware when your energy dips, and you are armed with a tool to *Tweak Your Speak*.

## "TAG" QUICKSHIFT™

When negative words jump out of your mouth, or negative thoughts just dropped into your mind:

1. **Breathe, smile, *Tag*, and forgive.** Breathe in and smile. As you exhale, lovingly say "Tag" to yourself and drop your shoulders. Forgiveness flows through your body.

2. **Take your time to locate kind, forgiving words.** Re-phrase what you said or what just came to mind.

## PROGRESS CONFIRMATION

You're nearly halfway there. You have experienced your fifth MindShift Exercise™ *Tag*. To remind you what you have learned, I suggest you intentionally say the following aloud:

> *"I am further taking control of my mind and creating the life I want, now that I have added Tag to my MindShift Toolbox™, which helps me monitor and shift away from negative thoughts and self-defeating words."*

## UP NEXT...

In the next chapter, I'll show you how to shift your mindset and body to neutral. Since I mentioned "shifting to neutral" several places in this chapter, your next MindShift Exercise™ *Shift Into Neutral* is perfectly timed. You'll learn how to "idle within neutral" rather than over-revving your engine and blowing a gasket.

# CHAPTER 9
## SHIFT INTO NEUTRAL (MSE 6)

In this chapter, your sixth MindShift Exercise™ is *Shift INTO Neutral*. Even the name of this exercise is calming to me. The process is simple and direct.

When aware, this method gives you the ability to neutralize your negative mindset, and in concert, take a mental vacation. Imagine this process as being your highway rest stop anywhere on the road you've chosen to travel.

Of course, you understand the importance of awareness. I'm sure you've noticed that the vast majority of people travel through life on auto pilot—reacting to what is happening—rather than taking purposeful action. At the same time, it seems some people have their gears stuck perpetually in reverse.

Consider. Are we born unmindful? How do we get sucked into a dismal rut and continue to speed forward without even looking for a way out?

The exit is not outside of you. Your way is deep within.

## HEAR MY VOICE

Right now, take a deep, slow breath with me. Hold for a moment. As you exhale with a smile on your face, sigh out loud, *"Ahhhhh."*

Again, breathe with me. This time as you exhale and sigh, *"Ahhhhh,"* physically drop your shoulders to release the tension in your body.

I just felt the shift. I hope you did as well.

Yet, there is a glitch when we just *shift TO neutral* rather than *shift INTO neutral*. I originally named the exercise *Shift TO Neutral*, however, that title missed the target. *Shift INTO Neutral* sets the proper intention for the exercise.

## THE PROBLEM

Shifting to neutral can be soothing. However, when I first envisioned being the driver, I mentally reached out, grasped my shiny, red gearshift knob, and shifted from one gear, to another, to another. I began to speed-shift right past neutral without lingering in neutral to take a mental break.

As a git-er-done gal, I was conditioned to get to the finish line *fast*, rather than enjoy the journey. For decades I had been MindShifting like a race car driver speed-shifting, yet I was missing the vital key to shifting my mindset. I was attached to speed. Like a fast food junkie, *"I wanted it; I wanted it my way; and I wanted it NOW!"*

I was preoccupied with running the gears. My mind was consumed with arriving at the destination. Frequently, I further compounded stress and neglected safety by multitasking in my mind.

I forgot to pull over and take a break. I failed to embrace the stillness that comes from remaining *inside* neutral.

## SPEED-SHIFTING AROUND YOU

In 2015, Microsoft began using the term "speed shift" in relation to personal computers running faster by upgrading to Windows 10. If you're a Mac user, just as my husband is, please bear with me.

In order to ramp up the speed of your computer with the upgrade, you also had to have an up-to-date Intel processor. The installable system (Windows 10) and the hardware (the processor) worked hand-in-hand, one boosting the other.

The computer's brain is its system software—in this instance, Windows 10. The computer's body part that interconnects and functions with the brain is the processor—in this case, the Intel processor.

Here's the gotcha. Once people started installing Windows 10, glitches started popping up. The computer's software-hardware connection was struggling, failing to correctly and fluidly complete functions.

Finally, Microsoft went out of their way to say, "Good news is coming to Windows 10 soon… in the form of a new patch."

*Seriously?* A major system upgrade immediately needed a software patch!

## WHAT HAPPENED?

Without having the proper system in place, moving too fast results in under-performing. That's exactly what was happening with Windows 10.

Thankfully, while standing in line at an electronics store, I heard a savvy computer geek say, "Wait! Let other people install Windows 10, and give Microsoft time to work out the bugs." I listened and waited.

Computer glitches happen all around us. They are oftentimes difficult to troubleshoot, locate, and fix. Glitches are usually 'transient faults' that correct themselves and seldom leave clues about their source. Sometimes you'll see a spinning wheel in the center of your computer screen while you impatiently wait for the computer to continue.

Many people were sidetracked in 2015 by technology glitches that...

- ...delayed hundreds of Southwest airline flights during the course of one day
- ...potentially mis-scored thousands of student exams in Indiana
- ...made it impossible to get a driver's license in Colorado for a few hours

I often wonder if software engineers are pushed so hard to finish coding, they have little time to test drive programs... *"Just get back to work and get it done. Now!"*

The result? Think of me as being the *MindShift Tester* for over half a century. While studying and creating MindShifting, I would ask myself, *"What is working correctly? What might need changing? How do I tweak the shift?"*

Sometimes, my mind-body-spirit connection experienced glitches, just like when my heart was out of rhythm and got worse. When I rooted out the cause—*fueling the fear*—I was able to rewrite the code by shifting away from fear and resetting.

## PROGRESS

For years, when I *shifted to neutral*, I experienced only a temporary, fleeting shift. I was calm for a split second, then I went right back to being out of balance and scattered. I had experienced a glitch.

*Cancel!*

Phew. Glad my internal, remote control is only a thought away.

The method had a glitch, not me. I wasn't defective. I had overlooked the importance of grounding and energetically connecting with Mother Earth.

Microsoft needed a patch to fix a glitch in Windows 10. I needed a patch to fix a MindShift Exercise™ glitch.

## THE ASKING TRAP

I asked myself, *"How do I create a patch for Shift To Neutral?"*

Whenever you want an answer, simply ask yourself a question, and let it go. Ask your question once, then listen for the answer.

For many years, I continued asking without listening and got trapped in the *asking-do-loop*. I'd ask repeatedly. Ask, then ask again. Ask just one more time. Maybe no one's listening. I continued asking the same question over and over, more often than any sane, logical person could stomach.

That may have happened to you, as well.

Think about this. How do you order an item online? Do you place the order and wait for the package to arrive? Or, do you place the order, receive confirmation, log back on and place the same order again?

Of course not. You place the order once and wait. Sometimes impatiently, but you wait. My husband once admitted that he had inadvertently placed the same online order twice.

In fact, my husband became involved in what I call the "Asking Trap" and got what he had asked for. Our six pack of four-pawed babies had dwindled down to two. During our family TV time, one pup sat with me and the other with mom.

My husband missed having a dog with him on his recliner so much, he kept saying he wanted a new dog to sit with him. He repeated himself over and over again.

Subsequently, we acquired three pups over eighteen months. All three now briefly visit with mom and me, then, jump into my husband's lap and play musical chairs.

Today, it's easier for me to ask once and get right back to whatever I'm doing. While thinking about *Shift To Neutral*, I asked, *"How do I create a patch?"*

Immediately, I got back to writing the following *Ask and Listen* section about asking a question. Below that section, I'll share how quickly the answer to creating a patch for this MindShift Exercise™ arrived.

Yes, there are often twists and turns getting to any answer. That's life's highway. Hairpin curve. Switchback. Detour. Straightaway. Sometimes you encounter a dead end and have to turn around and go back.

Asking a question often guides us by triggering relevant, related questions to pinpoint the answer. For me, the process is similar to masterminding with other people, being nudged this way, then that way without judgment. Rather than continually repeating the original question, just go with the flow.

## ASK AND LISTEN

Some people believe when you ask yourself a question, you're asking the Universe. Shortly, answers come back from the Universe in odd ways—bumps, sounds, visual cues, words, even people showing up or calling you.

Others believe when you ask yourself a question, you're asking your subconscious mind. Answers will come as thoughts float up into your conscious mind from the stores of information and experiences you had recorded and filed away.

After writing those two paragraphs, I wondered, "Which am I?"

My first thought made me chuckle again, *"You're a hybrid. You believe answers come from both directions—from the Universal library in the sky and from your own subconscious mind."*

I shifted my focus. That very moment, I started thinking about a hybrid car, which uses an internal combustion engine along with an electric motor powered by a set of batteries. Energy is stored in the fuel for the engine and in the electric batteries for the motor.

Energy is the fuel for our mere existence. I thought about plugging a hybrid car into an electric outlet, as well as using solar panels to recharge the batteries.

I asked another question, *"What is a different way to replenish batteries' energy?"*

Jumping on the Internet, I discovered that hybrid on-board batteries can also recharge inside the system. The batteries capture kinetic energy that is created when using the brakes, commonly referred to as "regenerative braking."

Now that's right up my alley! Regenerate, renew, restore, and reclaim. Revitalize.

Kinetic, or moving energy, directly mirrors using subtle body movements to shift and recharge your energy. This intrigued me.

Here's the key. In a hybrid car, the electric motor requires no energy while the car stops and remains idle. The electric engine literally stops using energy just as if it turned itself off.

Sounds like that is exactly where we want to be. Idling. Detached. Outside noise turned off. Consuming no energy.

Ah-hah! Idling while in neutral and recharging is clearly energy efficient for cars and certainly healthy for our mind and body.

There you have it. I asked and got the answer.

## THE SHIFT PATCH

Notice the name change when *Shift To Neutral* became *Shift Into Neutral.* Look at the words. Where is the changed word? In the middle.

What does "Into" mean? *"… within, inside, amid, among, in the middle of."*

That's the answer: Settle into your calm while you are inside neutral!

Reclaim your energy. Plug in. Recharge and repair. Revitalize your mind and your body.

You can quickly shift to level ground and settle into calmness, as opposed to fitfully gunning it full throttle, mentally and physically crashing into one barrier after another. Your new skillset will show you how to detach as you safely idle while resting inside neutral. Be there and be aware.

## REMINDER. WHY MINDSHIFTING WORKS

As you know, our mind-body connection is real. The state of our mind affects our body, and by reversing the current of the mind-body connection to body-mind connection, we use our body to shift our state of mind.

When we focus on using the body to shift our mindset by using subtle body movements, the process is more effective and much faster than just trying to think positive thoughts. Since MindShifting engages our body along with our mind, the more physical senses we have involved in any exercise, the more successful we are at deliberately shifting our mental gears. It is that simple.

**Ground Rule Reminder:** When you're stressed, overwhelmed or mentally fractured behind the wheel in your business or in your personal life, take a few minutes to recharge your batteries. Find a safe place and shift. Regardless of what you're doing, you deserve *me-time.*

## PREPARE TO SHIFT

*Shift Into Neutral* has become my handy-on-the-go-tool that is just a thought away. This exercise is a great way to center yourself at your core. The 9-step Details guide you through the experience and are deliberately thoughtful. The 4-step QuickShift™ is just that. Quick.

## SET YOUR INTENTION

The following intention is an effective way to prime your mind and body to shift. I recommend including this intention in your MindShifting ritual on a daily basis and whenever you receive an alert from your Energetic Radar.

> *"My intention is to shift to the moment and open my mind, body and spirit in preparation to shift my mindset."*

Let's begin.

## "SHIFT INTO NEUTRAL" DETAILED STEPS

**Step 1: Close your eyes. Breathe. Clutch. Roll to a safe stop in gear.**

Sit comfortably in your chair. Put your feet flat on the floor. Close your eyes. Take a couple of slow, deep breaths.

You are the driver. As your car rolls to a stop, move your left foot and easily push in the clutch.

Your car stops on level ground, safely away from all traffic. The emergency brake automatically engages.

Your car idles in gear with the clutch in. You are safe. Idling. Breathe naturally.

### Step 2: Look to the right, notice your gearshift. Touch and feel.

With your eyes closed, turn your head to the right and look slightly down at the gearshift. What does your gearshift look like? What is the knob's color?

Physically move your right hand. Reach over to the right and touch the gearshift knob. Move your fingers around the knob. Feel it.

What is its temperature? Is it cool, like a chrome knob, or warm to touch, like a leather-bound knob?

What is its form? Is it round? Oval? Or form-fitted to your hand?

Bring your hand back to your lap as if it's floating. Settle and breathe.

### Step 3: Become one with your gearshift.

Move your hand back over to your right and become one with your gearshift. As you move your hand over and around the gearshift knob, it takes the form of your hand, a perfect fit. The knob changes shapes and melds with your hand. Naturally.

At this very moment, you realize that you have full control, shifting your mental gears. The shifting mechanism is now an extension of you. It is within you.

Consciously inhale slowly and exhale softly. Feel your hand float back to your lap. Sit there in the joy, idling.

**Step 4: Reach to the right and shift INTO neutral.**

Physically reach back to your right and relax your arm. Your hand hovers just over the gearshift knob. As your hand glides down to the knob, the gearshift becomes part of your hand... now, your arm... then, your body.

Gently close your hand and move the gearshift knob into neutral. Feel the movement of the gearshift while it is in neutral and notice the range of motion.

Drop your shoulders. Release all the stress in your body and your mind. Settle into calmness as you shift into neutral.

**Step 5: Place your shift hand on your head.**

Inhale slowly and sit up straight. Comfortable. Completely at ease. Gently exhale.

Place the palm of your right hand on the top of your head. Position your hand back towards the crown of your head in line with your spine, rather than forward towards your forehead.

Rest your palm very lightly on your head. Take a deep breath through your nose and slowly breathe out through gently pursed lips.

**Step 6: Softly grasp your hair. Pull up and feel your body straighten.**

Continue to breathe deeply and fully as you close your right hand. Softly grasp a handful of your hair. Gently pull upward. Keep the mild tension on your hair and pull upward.

If you don't have hair, or if your hair is cut very short, imagine you are gently pulling your hair upwards. If you have no arms, or are unable to move your arms, or choose to remain physically still, visualize you are gently pulling your hair upward with your hand.

Notice how your hair feels in your hand. The texture. Notice where your hair connects to your scalp.

As you gently pull, feel your body straighten. Lift upward with each deep breath. Go up, and up, and up as you breathe.

**Step 7: Connect the Golden Cord.**

Imagine a golden cord going from the top of your head raising you upwards, gently elongating your neck and opening the spaces running down your spine. Hold that image for a few heart beats.

In your mind's eye, see your golden cord going deep inside your body, through your core, down your legs, into and out your feet. From the sole of each foot, your golden cord extends down and out deep into Mother Earth. You are plugging into the energy field of the earth. You are now grounded and fully connected.

You are idling within neutral; your batteries nearly fully charged. You're almost there. Your charge is at 90%… 91… 92…

**Step 8: Your arm floats to your side. You become fully charged.**

Allow your arm to float easily to your side. As your hand settles into your lap, smile broadly and give an audible sigh, "Ahhhhh," and feel your shoulders drop as well.

Relax your shoulders even more and allow any remaining tension to evaporate from your body. Feel your body melt into a puddle of pure relaxation.

Your batteries are at 97%… 98… 99.

You are comfortably resting within neutral, fully charged 100%, and ready to begin.

Open your eyes. You are calm and comfortable. Your batteries are charged. Sit for a few moments and luxuriate where you are.

## Step 9: Ask, "Where would I rather be?"

Look up and to the right. Pivot your body 45 degrees to the right. Continue looking up and ask, "Where would I rather be?"

You can either: Get up and get going, lie down and take a nap, or get a full night's sleep. Right now you decide. You are ready for anything.

## POST SHIFT REMINDER

Why is it important to be *within* neutral? When you are relaxed and revitalized, you can make better decisions, smarter life choices, and perform at your highest level.

Congratulate yourself for releasing that which no longer serves you. Sit and simply be in the moment. Sit there and just be.

## CASE STUDY

After learning *Shift Into Neutral*, one of our clients said, "This is a break-through concept for me. It allows me to move into any of several MindShift Exercises™ easily and completely."

Following is a brief portion of a coaching session with the same client. He moved away from being fearful because of stress to a place of joy, peace and excitement.

> **Donna:** *"When worry drops into your mind, what will you do?"*
>
> **Client:** *"Smile first. Engage my Energetic Radar and shift into neutral."*
>
> **Donna:** *"Tell me about your experience."*
>
> **Client:** *"I'm having a lot of fun and have something to look forward to. Instead of being an old fashion gun, flint lock that*

*scatters, I have a focused target. I'm excited about my future now that I've learned how to shift my mindset!"*

## "SHIFT INTO NEUTRAL" AT-A-GLANCE

1. **Close your eyes.** Breathe. Depress clutch. Roll to a safe stop while still in gear. Emergency brake automatically comes on.

2. **Look to the right, notice your gearshift.** Get acquainted. Touch and feel.

3. **Become one with your gearshift.** The gearshift knob conforms to your hand and fits perfectly.

4. **Reach to the right and shift *INTO* neutral.** Feel the loose space within neutral. Drop your shoulders. Release all your stress.

5. **Place your shift hand on your head.** Rest your hand in line with your spine.

6. **Softly grasp your hair.** Pull up and feel your body straighten. Your spine seems to breathe and open.

7. **Connect the Golden Cord.** Upward into the Universe and plugged deep within the earth's energy.

8. **Your arm floats to your side.** You are fully charged.

9. **Ask, *"Where would I rather be?"***

**Want to Recharge Faster?** When you need a mind-body shift and only have a brief moment to spare, *Shift Into Neutral* using the quicker version that follows. This QuickShift™ is a 4-step process.

**Even Faster?** By practicing often and fully grasping the concept of shifting *INTO* the calmness of neutral, you have created a healthy habit. After the process becomes natural, consider shifting directly into neutral using only two steps from the QuickShift™ version below, #1 and #4.

## "SHIFT INTO NEUTRAL" QUICKSHIFT™

1. **Close your eyes and breathe deeply.** Level ground. Safe. Reach over and shift into neutral.

2. **Gently grasp your hair.** Lift up and open your spine.

3. **Connect the Golden Cord.** Upward into the Universe and plugged deep within the earth.

4. **Settle into your calm.** Rest there idling WITHIN neutral as you recharge your batteries.

## RESULTS

By itself, this simple shift can, in fact, neutralize the stress in your body and help you refocus your mindset. You can move completely away from things you're fretting about, away from the fact that you just screwed up, and bring your mind back to what is important— *the now.*

This process moves you away from continually holding onto mental garbage. You have the power to intentionally release your residual head trash, gear up and begin again.

## PROGRESS CONFIRMATION

Since you've experienced your sixth MindShift Exercise™ *Shift Into Neutral,* you're halfway finished test-driving a dozen, different methods. Look back and Shift Into Neutral to savor what you have learned.

Before you move on, I suggest you intentionally say the following aloud:

> *"I am taking time for myself and creating the life I want, now that I can naturally Shift Into Neutral to counter-balance negativity while taking a mental vacation and recharging my batteries."*

## UP NEXT...

In the next chapter, I'm going to share a personal story about how I dealt with bullying growing up. Because I'm 6-foot 5-inches tall, you might think I was the bully. My experience will give you a different perspective.

People feel like victims when they are bullied. When you see yourself as the victim, you empower the bully by becoming the victim. When you are bullied, there is a way to sidestep and become stronger by shifting your mindset a particular way.

*Blow the Bully Away* is your next MindShift Exercise™. Read on and discover how your bully solution is just a puff away.

# Chapter 10
## Blow the Bully Away (MSE 7)

In this chapter, you'll find your seventh MindShift Exercise™ *Blow the Bully Away*, which is extremely personal to me. I experienced bullying at a young age. Since I'm 6-feet 5-inches tall (6-feet-5, 6'5", 1.96 meters), you might think I was the bully. The opposite is true.

When you hear someone say, "I had growing pains," you might believe growing pains are symbolic, never real. Again, the opposite is true. Physical growing pains are indeed real, and in their own way, they can become the bully.

Before I share the turmoil I experienced because I grew so fast and how bullying mentally devastated me, I want you to know who was, and still is, uplifting in my life. It is my mother. She helped me learn to love myself and overcome self-doubts.

### MOTHER IS MY TOUCHSTONE

Mother was raised on a farm during the Great Depression. She helped me shift both my mindset and my body. Without suggesting

Mother used any specific method, she did what came naturally to her.

Earlier in the *Tag* chapter, I mentioned that Mother automatically changed one word that clearly took root and grew into my belief today: *"The words we choose set ourselves up for either success or failure."*

While reading a children's book to me, Mother saw, "I *think* I can," and said, "I *know* I can." She spoke from her gut and guided with her heart. Thankfully, she still does that today.

She was a young mother, only 23 years my senior. She was smart, forgiving, and caring to everyone, not just me. She was extraordinary, and my schoolmates always asked her to accompany us on trips. Throughout high school, my mother was the chaperone-of-choice!

Mother still passes along her loving, earth-connected energy that people need every day. I'm grateful she came to share our home in 2002. I love doing quick videos of *Mama Peggy in Her Garden* talking about how to grow this, or that, or what's blooming.

When I upload a video of Mom from my smart phone to Facebook, she has more views and *likes* in an hour than anything else I've ever posted! My friends keep telling me to get a YouTube channel and website for Mama Peggy to keep her wisdom for posterity.

When I was eight, Mom went to night school on Wednesdays to learn secretarial and business skills, such as typing, bookkeeping and office management. She took me with her, gave me a quarter, and dropped me off at the movie theater in Big Stone Gap, Virginia, while she went to class.

I felt safe and secure in the theater, because I truly was. She knew the owners and, unknown to me, they watched over me.

When I think back over those years, I realize Mother was my role model and coach. Growing so much in a short period of time made it physically painful to straighten up, and I slouched a lot.

I remember Mother's wise counsel. When she caught me slumping, she would say, "Head up. Shoulders back. Stand up straight. Stick 'em out and be proud!"

"Yes, ma'am," I replied and stood up straight. Ironically, I had nothing to stick out until I was 30. Until then, I looked more like an awkward, 16-year-old boy.

While in high school, Mother even put Papa's back brace on me as a physical trigger to prompt me to straighten up when my shoulders went forward. In my twenties, I discovered that taking immediate and continual action by shifting my body frame during my teen years had been miraculous. Literally, I had completely straightened a severe, curvature deformity in my spine that I didn't even know existed.

Thankfully, I was blessed. My growth was natural, genetically based. Without any malfunctioning glands—like the pituitary, or any disease that triggers unnatural bone growth—I am the healthy result of my gene pool.

## "BUTT UP"

My heart goes out to everyone who dislikes their body or who they are. If you have lowered your self-esteem and detest your height, your weight, your looks, the color of your skin, your sexual orientation, your ethnic origin, or whatever... pay attention: *You are bullying yourself!*

Listen closely to my words:

*"Get your butt up! Hold your head high. Shoulders back. Stand up straight. Stick 'em out and be proud."*

Oh, okay. That was Mother-speak. I added, *"Get your butt up!"* That part was me talking.

Just do it right now. Get up out of your chair, off your couch, out of your bed and buck up. Take a moment to rejoice and love yourself.

## GROWING PAINS BULLIED ME

Regardless of the source, growing pains are real. There are verifiable, physical and mental growing pains. They naturally intertwine, one fertilizing the other, which clearly illustrates our body-mind-spirit connection at work.

My growing pains were physically based and heightened by emotional strife. No pun intended.

By the time I was twelve, I was taller than most other kids my age. In a short while, I was taller than all my teachers, my brother and both my parents.

My brother is three years older than me. When he was in the ninth grade, I zoomed right past him. I think we were the same height for two short weeks.

Since I grew nine inches in one year, rather than being abstract, my growing pains were real. Bones can naturally grow faster than soft tissue, which is exactly what happened to me. Acute strain on my ligaments and tendons produced genuine physical pain, deep inside my body.

While my pain was physically created, agony was amplified by how my mindset handled emotional and mental trauma. My mindset was fragile and fragmented. Mental warfare came along, but I was a child—an unseasoned warrior.

I grew up fast... in more ways than one.

## BULLY'S POWER SOURCE

In the fifth grade, I was bullied mercilessly. I began the year an even 5-foot tall and grew seven inches during the school year. My life was tilted, out of balance.

I grew so fast, everything seemed to move from one week to the next—door knobs, toilet seats, you name it. They moved. I felt like life was picking on me. People, too.

In particular, a tough, burly school girl, who was nearly six inches shorter than me, kept getting in my face, so to speak. She physically pushed and shoved me repeatedly. She was violent during recess and dared me to push back. She threatened me, and said if I pushed back, she would tell everyone, *"Donna is soooo BIG, SHE started it!"*

Rather than stand up for myself, I slinked away. I held my head down and felt belittled.

Looking back I realize I initially felt victimized. I clearly remember the question I asked myself over and over again, *"Why do I deserve being treated like this?"*

My words sabotaged me. The way I asked myself questions handed the controls over to the bully. It took years for me to clearly understand what empowers a bully:

- When someone bullies you, you give them authority by slipping into the victim mindset. That's where bullies get their power—from you. A bully's control is strengthened when you become the victim and ask yourself questions like this, "Why am I being treated this way?"
- You always look for excuses and give your mind the wrong questions to answer. When you feed yourself unhealthy questions, more darkness is imprinted on your subconscious.

## SIDESTEP THE BULLY

One day I physically sidestepped the bully's attack. She lost balance, stumbled and fell flat on her face. She was flustered. She blurted out unclear words. Directly in front of me, she appeared to physically shrink in size.

The tension suddenly left my body. I felt relief and naturally dropped my shoulders, which sparked an instant MindShift. Titling my head, a fleeting smile crossed my lips. My eyes slightly narrowed, and I thought, *"Hmm... how did THAT happen?"*

Inside my head, my thoughts traveled at lightning speed. As she literally seemed to get smaller and fade away, my fear of abuse transformed to puzzlement, then instantly turned into a type of wonderment.

I no longer felt like a victim! I shifted away from being the victim to becoming the observer. As if by magic, I became detached.

Whenever I recall that moment, it makes me smile. I wonder if by chance, what took place back then became the seed for my MindShift Exercise™ *Hmm... Isn't That Interesting?*

The following summer, I added another two inches of growth making me nine inches taller in twelve short months. The resulting physical growing pains made another shift in my perspective.

## SERIOUS GROWING PAINS

Since my body had grown so fast, the physical pain was crippling. As I mentioned, bones can grow faster than the ligaments, tendons and muscles that hold our skeleton together. My soft connective tissue needed time to catch up to my bone growth.

When I walked at a normal pace, I felt like someone was stabbing an ice pick in my heel and up into the arch of my foot. It was piercing, splintering pain. White lights flashed in my head with each step.

When Mother took me to the doctor, he said the only solution to stop tearing the Achilles tendon was to give my soft tissue time to catch up to my bone growth. He prescribed elevated shoes to take pressure off the tendon.

How fun was that? Ironic, maybe.

Going into the sixth grade at 5-feet 9-inches tall, I wore black, lace-up shoes with 2-inch thick heels just like my Grandma's dress shoes. You heard me right.

Classy platforms for kids didn't exist in 1961. I stuck out like a sore thumb and stood eye-to-eye with my teacher.

## TIME FLEW BY

By the time I graduated from high school, I thought I had stopped growing and was a tad over 6-feet 4-inches tall. During the summer between junior and senior year, I ran for Governor at Virginia Girls State, sponsored by the American Legion Auxiliary. My campaign slogan was "*Six feet four. Who could ask for more?*"

Who asked? Not me. But I did win the election.

When I was twenty-two, I measured 6-feet 5-inches. Subsequently, I expanded my slogan: "*Six foot four. Who could ask for more? Now I'm six foot five. Glad to be alive!*"

## "BLOW THE BULLY AWAY" DETAILED STEPS

**Intention:** To stop feeling and being bullied; to stop handing over the power to the bully.

**When to Use:** You are on emotional tilt, off center. You feel as if one particular person is gunning for you, or you feel like everyone is out to get you. You are at home, at work, in a social setting or competing in a sporting event. You lost your power and feel weak.

## HOW TO BLOW THE BULLY AWAY

This is a fun and empowering MindShift Exercise™ that fully engages both your body and mind. Just like other methods, it takes much longer to explain than to do in real time. Integrating the process into your MindShifting practice enables you to create your own shorthand version. Take your time reading through each step. For many, *Blow the Bully Away* is profound.

## MINDSET SCALE™

Just as we did with *Hmm... Isn't That Interesting?*, go through the rating process before and after you *Blow the Bully Away*, then compare the shift. How much did your baseline number change?

If there is no change, that is okay, too. Sometimes, what we are focusing on is different than what is troubling us. The simple process helps calm our mind so the underlying situation will eventually float to the surface.

By using numbers, we shift over to left-brain thinking, which gives us a logical way to measure and verify the results. Using mental imaging, we engage the creative aspect of our brain's right hemisphere.

## RATE IT REMINDER

- **Baseline:** Bring a bullying situation to mind. Rate where you are right now. How do you feel? 0-10?
- **Finish line:** When you step through the process, once again, rate where you are. How are you feeling? 0-10?
- **Shift Results:** What is the difference? (Baseline minus finish line)

**BASELINE**

Take a moment and imagine someone bullying you, or how life continues to push you around without letting up. Zero is nothing. 10 is the worst. Write down where you are now. Set that aside.

Let's begin.

**Step 1: Close your eyes. Breathe and release.**

To begin, close your eyes, put your feet flat on the floor, sit comfortably, and take three slow deep breaths. Inhale and hold for a few moments. As you exhale through gently pursed lips, drop your shoulders and release the tension.

Notice the air as it travels in through your nose and down into your body. As you breathe, the air makes its way into and out of your lungs. Listen to the subtle change in the sound as the air moves.

The simple process of doing, listening, and noticing, brings you back to the moment and raises your awareness.

You are now the driver. You have the steering wheel in your hands.

**Step 2: With eyes closed, open your body.**

Softly hold out your hands in front of you, palms up. Your elbows are bent and rest comfortably at your sides.

As you breathe in deeply, hold and feel sunlight on your body, warming your face, chest, and hands.

Exhale slowly through pursed lips. Once again, gently drop your shoulders.

**Step 3: Open your eyes. Inspect your hands. Make fists. Open and close your hands and notice the differences.**

Pull your hands near your face so you can see them clearly. Notice their shape, their color. Turn your hands over and around and look

133

at all the sides of your hands. Look at the valleys and peaks on your knuckles.

As you breathe slowly in, make a fist with both hands and squeeze tightly. Notice the color drain from your fingers and your knuckles. Feel your fingernails gently touching the palms of your hands.

Release your fists as you exhale and softly hold your hands open. Notice the color come back into your hands and fingers as the blood returns.

Once again, breathe in and make a tight fist with both hands. Hold the fists and turn your hands over and around, noticing where the color has left, how tight your skin is, and how your fingers are squeezed together.

Notice how your body feels holding clenched fists. As you release your fists, open both hands and hold them softly in front of you.

Make breathing sounds as you slowly and forcefully exhale through pursed lips. Feel your cheeks puff out.

Gently lift your body. Yet again, drop your shoulders.

**Step 4: Left hand floats to lap and rests there. Make fist with right hand. Release and relax into a gently rocking cradle.**

Let your left hand float gently back to your lap. Make a fist with your right hand. Rather than grasping and holding on, release your right hand and slowly open it, palm side up.

Stretch your fingers wide apart. As you notice the space between your fingers, put a bit more space between your fingers.

Relax your hand. As you hand floats in front of you, it reminds you of a gently rocking cradle.

**Step 5: Close your eyes. Ask the bully to show itself, take form, and step up into your hand. Define it.**

Visualize the bully standing in front of you, face-to-face. It might be female, male, or it might be you. The bully might even be a snarling creature. Detach and observe. As you say, "Hmm…," the bully begins to shrink.

Slowly lower your open palm and ask the bully to step up, into your hand. At first your hand is heavy, and you feel the weight of the bully in your hand. Your arm and hand may even drop ever so slightly as you feel yourself fight to hold your ground.

But wait. The bully is shrinking further down. You notice as it becomes smaller and smaller and smaller. Hold your hand softly.

**Step 6: Hand floats to your face. Disconnect then "*Hmm-It*" and "*Heart-It.*"**

Keeping your eyes closed, the bully cradled in your hand becomes even smaller. Your hand floats towards your face.

Hold your hand softly near your chin and mouth so you can get a closer look at the bully. Cradle it gently. Notice its smallness; notice how tiny.

Naturally smile. Completely disconnect and say, "*Hmm… isn't that interesting?*"

As you think this thought, "How cute and helpless," breath in, smile. Send love from your heart to its heart center.

If you feel uncomfortable, or if sending love to the bully feels unnatural, of course that's okay. Just imagine cartoon hearts floating from your body and hovering over the itsy, bitsy bully who sits in the palm of your hand. Watch as the cartoon hearts melt and flow down and around the bully's tiny body.

## Step 7: Now, huff and puff.

Blow the bully out of the palm of your hand. Send it away with blessings for a fulfilling life; just take it someplace else, out of your sight.

Puff! Gently blow the bully away, just like a child blowing a feather, a piece of dandelion fluff, or soap bubbles. Watch as the bully floats away on the air. Watch with childlike curiosity, wondering how far the bully will land away from you.

Smile, take a breath. Inhale, huff, and puff and blow. The bully floats away.

## Step 8: Open your eyes and celebrate.

You have now blown the bully away! Open your eyes and look at your empty hand. The bully is gone. Clap your hands. Applaud and cheer.

### Shift Results

Now that you have blown the bully away, rate it. Revisit the bully situation you brought to mind before you started. Where are you right now? How do you feel? 0-10?

What is the difference? What was your before-number, and what is it now? How has your *Mindset Scale*™ changed?

### CASE IN POINT

In the fifth grade when I thought, *"I am being bullied,"* guess what, I was. By thinking you are being bullied in any area of your life, you energetically become weaker and give the controls over to another person or to a situation.

When the pushy, school girl stumbled and fell, my sidestep shifted my physical position from confrontation to letting conflict go by. The ripple effect of my body-mind connection shifted the way I was feeling from being bullied to noticing what was happening and becoming the detached observer.

Think about that possibility in your life right now. Sidestepping can work wonders on multiple levels—whether within the office hierarchy or on the family front, avoiding simple mistakes to dealing with power struggles can be life-changing.

## SUGGESTED MISSIONS

Take a moment and reflect on what surrounds you. What's going on in your profession, your trade, your retirement, your relationships, your family, or in any part of your life? Notice the changes—what kind and how much.

Right now, look back in time. Write down what has been going on around you. List the ups and downs outside of you that are out of your control.

Consider how you've performed and what you have accomplished. Are there people who push you around, shake your self-worth, and steal your self-confidence? From first-hand experience, I bet there are.

After this chapter, I want your biggest takeaway to become the QuickShift™ version so you can swiftly blow your bully away. The At-A-Glance gives you the shortened form with all eight steps.

**Smile at Fear:** Find your brave heart. You can stop struggling when someone bullies you. First, just stop bullying yourself. Then, huff and puff. You can blow the bully away with one simple breath.

## "BLOW THE BULLY AWAY" AT-A-GLANCE

1. **Close your eyes.** Breathe and release. Use 3-breath process and become aware.

2. **Eyes remain closed, open your body.** Hands softly resting, palms up, warmed by sunlight. Drop shoulder.

3. **Open your eyes.** Focus on hands. Make fists, open and notice. Repeat. Lift body. Drop shoulders again.

4. **Left hand floats to lap. Squeeze right hand tight into a fist.** Release and relax. Hand becomes a gently rocking cradle.

5. **Close your eyes. Ask bully to show itself.** The bully shrinks and steps into your hand.

6. **Hand floats to face. Bully in hand shrinks further.** Disconnect. Send love to its heart.

7. **Huff and puff.** Blow the bully away.

8. **Open your eyes and celebrate.** Look at your empty hand. Your bully is gone. Clap your hands. Applaud.

## WHY "IT" MATTERS

Below, notice the "it" within the QuickShift™. By simply revising how you notice "him, her, them, everyone or even life" to "it, its or itself", your WordShift™ dethrones the bully as well.

## "BLOW THE BULLY AWAY" QUICKSHIFT™

1. **Bully is in your hand.** It is shrinking.

2. **Detach** and observe it.

3. **Send love** from your heart to its heart.

**4. Huff & puff.** Blow it away.

## PROGRESS CONFIRMATION

Since you've experienced your seventh MindShift Exercise™ *Blow the Bully Away,* I suggest you intentionally say the following aloud:

> *"I am creating the life I want, now that I have sidestepped being the victim, stopped bullying myself, and learned how to lovingly Blow the Bully Away."*

## UP NEXT...

After the next chapter, I'll give you one of my favorite MindShift Exercises™ *The Egg,* which helps you automatically protect your energy fields while deflecting negative energy as opposed to absorbing it.

But first, there is another detour. Why? Because it is now time to take a mental break.

Look at where you are. What you have learned and how far you've come. Give the concepts and methods some time to settle and digest. Allow what you've added to your skillset to take root and anchor before we move on.

Remember, I'm your co-pilot sitting right beside you. Let's take a step-back together and look at how well you have created your own, personal MindShift Toolbox™. Re-adjust as you feel the need. It's your toolbox. You are the pilot.

The next chapter is full of yummy morsels. You'll want to add *"look back and mull it over"* to your road map.

# CHAPTER 11
## CHEW ON IT

Before you meet your eighth MindShift Exercise™ in the next chapter, take a *mental staycation*. Stay where you are, move to the moment, relax, and reflect on what you have learned.

Right now, rather than learn something new, chew a while. Ponder on where you are and what you've learned while celebrating how far you've come. Think about how you might use MindShifting in your life to change your perspective.

For me, our point of view is fluid, based on our experiences. We can step back, use logic and reasoning to massage and understand what we have learned. We gather information through our five, physical senses and combine that with the memory of all interactions, from both our conscious and subconscious mind.

### WHY CHEW A WHILE?

Harvard Business School published research in 2014 that makes my point. Regardless of how we learn best, we will make the greatest progress learning and accomplishing goals by spending time reflecting on our experiences.

"Reflecting" reminds me of "introspection," which has been a subject of philosophical discussion for thousands of years. It's comforting to see an Ivy League school jump on board and confirm the value of examining our own conscious thoughts and feelings.

Individual experience inside our own mind is unique and supremely our own. Reflection clearly becomes the teacher.

## AN ANCIENT MINDSHIFT SEED

The Greek philosopher Plato was the proverbial father of traditional Western philosophy. He asked, "Why should we not calmly and patiently review our own thoughts, and thoroughly examine and see what these appearances in us really are?"

Dang it! Pardon me for saying this—seriously, forgive me—but, why did Plato use "should" and "not" in many of his teachings?

Just sayin'.

Plato was a wise man and the founder of the first institution of higher learning in the Western world, the Academy of Athens. However, his words are "shoulding" on us, and by including "not" in many of his teachings, our mind becomes confused.

I wish Plato had thought about shifting his words. Maybe the following is what he meant, which is paraphrased in my own words:

> "Calmly and patiently review your own thoughts. Thoroughly reflect on what you are thinking so that you can clearly see what your thoughts mean, how your thoughts are creating your reality, and what lessons you can learn."

Plato's lifework is believed to have survived intact for over 2,400 years. I hope it's okay to tweak his words. Maybe, Plato is looking down, smiling and thinking, *"Why didn't I think of that?!"*

## HARVARD'S RESEARCH MENTIONED JOHN DEWEY

Harvard's research proceeded to quote an American philosopher, psychologist and educational reformer, John Dewey: "We do not learn from experience ... we learn from reflecting on experience."

I wholeheartedly agree with the concept, but, yet another use of the word "not. Despite his word choice, Dewey had a positive impact on our education system during his lifetime (1859-1952). He lived during the time the United States experienced cultural growing pains.

Just like my physical growing pains, the USA's pains were real. Our country developed from a simple, frontier-agricultural society to a complex, urban-industrial nation. Within that chaos, John Dewey believed the educational experience needed "continual reorganization, reconstruction and transformation of experience," which is clearly empowered by reflection.

Here's a thought that just came to my mind: "Life is chaos. When we mindfully, continually, and forgivingly reorganize and reconstruct our thought-patterns within chaos, we fluidly transform our own life by shifting our point of view."

That has way too many syllables. Let me try that again: "Shifting *into* neutral, the calmness inside our mind provides a safe place to reflect and gain perspective."

That's better. I like simple.

## CHEW ON WHAT?

Mother grew up on a farm, only fifteen miles from the coal mining camp where I was raised. As a child, I was fortunate enough to spend time on the farm with my Grandma, who taught me to appreciate and learn from nature. Reflecting back, I now realize that I learned more from Grandma than she might have envisioned.

Ever heard of "cows chewing the cud," what that means, and how long cows chew? If you've never heard the word "cud" before, cud sounds like mud. And, no, cows do not chew on mud.

Grandma taught me about the cud. Simply put, cows must chew their food twice in order to digest properly. "Chewing the cud" has morphed into a concept that continually helps me process what I learn and experience.

Even though cattle are big animals with horns, they lack agility and have limited defenses against predators. Part of cattle's genetic code tells them to eat quickly when they graze, then, go find a safe place and re-chew.

Cows *power eat.* They chew fast and gulp down their food. They chew just enough to moisten the food and swallow. This food goes into the first of their four-compartment stomach, mixes with digestive juices and becomes softer.

Next, they burp up partially digested food, the cud (a small ball of food), and chew it again. When they swallow, the re-chewed food goes into the next stomach compartment for further processing.

Humph! I wonder if we have cow-code hidden in our human DNA. When we eat, we often gulp and run. You might call that the "Fast Food Syndrome" that stresses our body and *conditions our mind to just hurry up,* rather than taking the time to ruminate what we just learned.

I love the word "ruminate" defined this way: "…think deeply about something, turn over in the mind, meditate or contemplate, mull over, ponder, chew on, puzzle over, and celebrate…"

## CHEW HOW LONG?

Cows chew their cud for eight hours a day, 30,000 to 40,000 chews! That's not merely one ball of burped-up food, but multiple small bites, chewed one at a time.

Generally, cows don't just stand around chewing the cud. They find a safe, protected comfortable place, lie down and chew away.

Recalling one steamy, hot summer on the farm with Grandma, I clearly remember a particular day as if it happened this afternoon. I'm sharing this memory to illustrate how using all five senses, combined with multiple strong feelings, can firmly anchor a memory. I vividly recall what happened in a two-minute time frame nearly six decades ago.

This memory recall is also intended to show you how easily you can learn and remember how to MindShift. While learning any method, engage all your senses and flavor with your feelings. Then, reflect and tweak as you go. In the process, you will end up with a toolbox filled with exercises that are uniquely yours.

As you read my genuine memory below, notice where all five of my senses were involved: sight, sound, smell, sense of touch, and taste. Also observe how thoughts, feelings, and experiences affected my perspective.

## MEMORY RECALL

*In my mind's eye, I'm walking across a hay field and vividly see a cow chewing her cud. She's lying beside a cool, bubbling brook in the shade, under a low hanging limb of an old tree. She leisurely chews and moves the bottom part of her mouth and chin, which looks like she is slowly grinding her food.*

*The hay was just cut and smells really good. The hay is raked into rows waiting to be baled. Stepping over a row, I stumble and fall down hard.*

*I scowl, look around, and whine, "Where did my sandal go?"*

*My arms are sweaty. I dust off the hay as I get up. A drop of water rolls into my left eye, and I blink. I lick my upper lip and taste salt.*

*"OUCH!" I swat at a bee that stings the outside of my right thigh. I pull the stinger out and hop around. My other sandal falls off, and I hurt both feet on the hay stubble.*

*Looking down at the sting near the bottom of my shorts, I wonder if the bee was going after those tiny, yellow flowers on my uncomfortable shorts. They keep rising up. I turn my head to the right as I reach back with my right hand and pull my shorts out of the crack of my butt.*

*I wonder, "Why are my shorts doing that? I just got them last month when summer started. They used to fit so good. Why are they shrinking?"*

*Looking back at the cow, thoughts flood my mind... about the cow... about what the cud tastes like... about how my clothes keep getting smaller... about how I need a pair of sandals that stay on... about how hot it is...*

## WHY SHARE THIS MEMORY

There are more ways to remember than by just using our five senses. Take a look at other memory anchors that were engaged during that two-minute walk across the hay field:

- Awareness of surroundings—temperature, sweat rolling down my face, uneven ground
- Physical movement—walking, stumbling, losing sandal, swatting the bee, hopping around, losing other sandal, turning head and tugging at shorts

- Physical pain—bee sting, hopping on hay stubble with bare feet
- Memory—recalling when I got the shorts
- Emotions—frustration, confused about growing, discomfort with clothing

By adding emotions, feelings, and physical movement to the mix, we have the recipe to help improve our memory and access any experience quicker. When we engage all of our senses, we raise the probability of anchoring what we want to remember and quickly retrieve.

Rather than reading any book non-stop from cover-to-cover, think about activating more of your senses. Consider pausing and reflecting on concepts that are new to you, or looking at something you already know in a different light.

However, when you're excited about the read and race to the end, here's an idea. Once you finish, go back to the beginning and start over to savor the ride.

Excitement energizes. Taking action helps to merge what you are learning with what you already know.

Find yourself a cozy place to reflect on what you've learned. At the end of a chapter, take some time to cogitate and digest. Evaluate how you can use MindShifting to improve your life.

Chew on that for a while.

## RINSE AND REPEAT

When I started coaching remotely by way of conference calls and webinars, I met with my clients three times each month during group sessions. Then, we took a week's break. Rather than a spring break, I called that time period an RMD, "Reflect. Massage. Digest."

During our RMD, you wait to learn something new while reflecting and practicing. You spend time looking back at your experiences and test drive different MindShift methods.

I've discovered that the "Reflect. Massage. Digest." philosophy with clients accelerated the effectiveness of coaching. "Slow down to go faster" sounds odd; however, this school of thought clearly helped me become a better coach. Subsequently, we changed group coaching to twice a month, separated by *mental staycations*.

## ROUTINE

My approach to everything in life has changed. After more than half a century searching for answers, the following is my overarching belief.

> *Taking time reflecting, rather than speed-shifting through any process, gives you the opportunity to contemplate and digest, transforming from a quick fix to a long-term solution. In the process, you create a sanctuary and playground for the mind, while giving you tangible ways to help change your life for the better.*

When you choose to integrate any MindShifting technique into your life, make it a routine—a habit. Any process practiced time and time again, will eventually become instinctive and a natural part of you.

You can effectively alter your DNA and underpin your life by setting clear intentions while balancing your mental, emotional, and physical wellbeing. Reflect on how well your MindShift Toolbox™ is coming together.

Consider the power you currently have at your fingertips. You are the driver, and the steering wheel is in your hands.

## REFLECT. MASSAGE. DIGEST.
### Creating Your MindShift Toolbox™

**Up to this point,** you have learned seven MindShift Exercises™. Think of this as your *Seventh Inning Stretch*, a simple process that comes from baseball. In the middle of the seventh inning, every baseball game comes to a stop. Everyone can literally stand up and stretch, sing an old song and take a breather.

The tradition helps to remind baseball players and fans of the game's roots, at the same time, it gives the players relief from their physically and mentally grueling game. I believe the Seventh Inning Stretch effectively is baseball players' shift into neutral where they breathe, take a few moments, and re-set.

Now, it's your turn. Spend some time reflecting, massaging, and digesting where you are and how far you've come. You might even want to put on your favorite music.

## SHIFT, REFLECT AND OWN IT

Shift from "me speaking heart-to-heart to you," to "you speaking lovingly to self." With intention, slowly read the following words aloud. If you're sitting in a public place, hear your voice inside your head, tenderly speaking to self.

*From My Point of View, I am Confirming My Progress.*
**I am creating the life I want, now that...**

1. **...I am taking control of my mind,** know how to shift my mindset with *Gear Up*, and have become the driver.

2. **...I have become the detached observer** with *Hmm... Isn't That Interesting?*, and I know when to ask myself the *Where* question that delivers *code modifiers* to my subconscious mind.

149

3. ...**I can gently reboot my mindset** with the *90-Second Shift*, which releases the stress from both my body and my mind.

4. ...**I have received my *Energetic Vaccine*** to avoid catching *Energetic Flu* and have installed and engaged my *Energetic Radar* to alert me when my internal energy shifts in the wrong direction.

5. ...**I am further taking control of my mind** by adding *Tag* to my toolbox, which helps me monitor and shift away from both negative thoughts and words that come to mind and jump out of my mouth.

6. ...**I am taking time for myself** where I can naturally *Shift Into Neutral*, to counter-balance any negativity that might arise, take a mental vacation and recharge my batteries.

7. ...**I have sidestepped being the victim**, stopped bullying myself, and learned how to lovingly *Blow the Bully Away*.

Take a moment and write down how you feel. What methods are the most comfortable and feel natural to you? Which methods would you like to go back and review later?

If you think you need more time to learn any technique, consider this. By writing down what you "think you need" you remove the "I-don't-know-how-to-do-that" from your *now-mind* and put that method on your "I'm-okay-I'll-do-that-later" list.

Writing down anything declutters your mind. *Making a list is the housekeeper of our mind.*

Now that IS interesting!

## BUILT-IN LIST

In the Appendix at the end of the book, you'll see the *MindShift Rolodex*—your built-in list of MindShift Exercises™. For easy access, you'll find a reference back to the chapter that introduced and explained each method along with its QuickShift™.

## UP NEXT...

In the next chapter, you'll find *The Egg*. The MindShift Exercise™ that helps you automatically protect your energy fields while deflecting negative energy as opposed to absorbing it.

Read on. Now is the time to meet your *Egg*.

# CHAPTER 12
# THE EGG (MSE 8)

Now that you've chewed a while, your eighth MindShift Exercise™ is *Put Your Egg On*. In short, it is *The Egg*.

Because of my deliberate focus on wellness rather than disease, I've shared *The Egg* with many individuals in the healthcare industry—with nurses, nurse managers, hospital staff, home healthcare aides, even medical doctors. I'm delighted how receptive Western medical professionals are to this particular method, especially since it's based on the Eastern philosophy of energy.

Topping the list for people from all walks of life are both *Hmm... Isn't That Interesting?* and *The Egg*. I often share these during LIVE events, on webcasts, in videos and workshops, on the radio, and from stage.

After a brief introduction to the concept of MindShifting, people often say, "I do feel better," or "This seems odd or unusual, but I can do that anyway," or "Isn't that cool," or "I'm going to use that right now!"

The following email tickled me:

> *"Thank you for a wonderful webinar, Donna... I've been studying these philosophies and practices for over 30 years, and I found your information clear and concise, unlike many of the so called 'gurus' who try to teach these concepts. Sometimes, understanding these ideas is like squeezing Jell-O—the harder you try to grasp it, the faster it runs away."*

Since I just told you this process is one of my "first-shares," in my head I heard you shouting, *"Why did you wait so long to share The Egg with ME in your book?!"*

## WHICH COMES FIRST

So, why didn't the *The Egg* come first?

Simple. I've been speaking to you from my heart.

Writing this book, I put my hat on as your executive coach. Since you are the king or queen of your life, I am your right hand, your trusted adviser. Rather than dash headlong into oddities, I wanted to lovingly guide you step-by-step through each method while laying a firm foundation.

In order to make lasting changes with MindShifting, I believe building a solid foundation must come first; just like shifting the gears of a car to neutral on safe, level ground, or pouring firm footers and foundations for homes and skyscrapers. The more attention you spend digging deep, and then, intentionally laying your MindShifting foundation, the more your mind-body-spirit connection will flourish and blossom over time.

I'll get to the details of *Putting Your Egg On* shortly. But first, I want to give you the gist of what to expect when using this method.

## YOUR EXPECTED OUTCOME

Results may vary. By the time you finish this chapter, hopefully, you will have "put on" your personal *Egg*. The purpose of *The Egg* is to insulate you from external negative energy, which bombards your energetic fields.

The mirrored, exterior surface of your *Egg* is a deflector that actively protects you from the unhealthy energy that continually invades your universe.

Think of your *Egg* as a flexible, multi-directional, bulletproof shield that continually protects all of you, without requiring that you remain consciously aware. Once you have installed your *Egg*, it will remain in place. However, you must promise yourself to routinely check your *Egg* for maintenance, just like you would with any other device.

Phew! That was a mouthful.

If "device" sounds too technical or mechanical, think about what you do after you put on business attire rather than comfortable, kickback clothing. Periodically, you might smooth your skirt or straighten your tie.

Okay, stop laughing. I only have one skirt, and my husband hasn't put on a tie in nearly two decades, but I know you get the point. You adjust a bit while you go through your day.

## RHYME TIME

The nursery rhyme, *Humpty Dumpty Sat On A Wall* by Mother Goose was the stimulus for the following verse I wrote. Hopefully, it gives you a smile.

*Without putting on The Egg, you fail to prepare.*
*As life pushes hard, you often shatter in despair.*
*When you put on your Egg designed to deflect, flex, and bend.*
*Your energy field is protected and won't crack wide open*
*again.*

## LAYING "THE EGG'S" SOLID FOUNDATION

No pun intended. "Laying" is certainly a play on words. Everything leading up to this chapter has laid the foundation for understanding the simplicity of *The Egg*.

Some people tell me *The Egg* is the MindShifting method they use the most. Even though energetic protection is a completely new concept to many people, they still use *The Egg*. Why? Because using their *Egg* helps them to feel better.

## WHEN "THE EGG" WORKS

Detach and think about negative situations you would like to avoid in the future. Rather than mentally dwelling on such conditions, create a profile. What did that feel like? Look like? Where did it occur? When and with whom?

For contrast, just take a glimpse rather than hop onto the emotional roller coaster. Then, let those thoughts go.

Consider the danger of allowing damaging energy to directly assault you. It happens all the time, especially around sick people, angry people, fractured people, greedy people, hateful people... The list goes on and on.

There are energetic vampires with fangs or buzzards with sharp talons. I've often envisioned these people having notoriously sharp teeth or razor-sharp claws that puncture, slice, and dice my energy field and suck the life right out of me.

Now, shift away from that image. Just writing about the concept gives me the creeps.

*Hmm... it is interesting* how energetically protecting self is beneficial while we are with family members we dearly love, as well as when we're in crowded spaces with people we know and care about. Regardless of our profound love, my husband, my Mom, and I periodically slip into our not-okay-place and lash out.

Fortunately, I've personally combined *The Egg* with *Hmm... Isn't That Interesting?* (Chapter 4) and *Tag* (Chapter 8) for decades, and my life keeps getting better. So does theirs.

Here are some other places where you might find *The Egg* uplifts how you feel:

- Stepping into an elevator
- Walking down a crowded street
- Entering a bustling mall with multitudes of people
- Going into a hospital to visit an ailing person

## WHAT HAPPENS WHEN YOU ARE THE PATIENT?

When you're sick, you can consciously protect your immune system. Yes, you can energetically shore up your own natural defenses, even when you are physically weak. Depending on what you hold in your mind, you can either protect or further damage yourself physically and mentally.

Think about the situation when you are the caregiver, constantly at the bedside of someone you love. Just like the individual being cared for, you are also at a higher risk of energetic invasion when around other sick people. Your jeopardy depends on where you focus.

## "PUT YOUR EGG ON" OVERVIEW

**Intention:** To protect your energy field while filtering out negativity and allowing perfectly aligned, loving energy to flow directly to you.

**How:** *The Egg* performs as both a filter and a deflector:

- As a filter, your *Egg* allows good thoughts, vibrations and energy to reach you. At the same time, the mirrored exterior surface deflects negative thoughts, emotions, and feelings.

- As a deflector, the *Egg's* mirror *selectively deflects only negativity* out into the cosmos where that energy becomes neutralized.

- If you were to *reflect negativity directly back to its source*, that action might create bad karma that comes back to haunt you.

Everything is energy. Our body is run by electricity, and all around your body is an energy field that you can touch and feel. It can even be photographed as well.

Our personal energy flows all around our body, unconfined by our skin. Our energy is tangible. With your hand, you can physically feel your energy field, just to the outside of your body. You can sense a slight resistance.

The size of our energy field outside our body is based on many factors: where we were raised, where we live now, our current emotions, our wellness, and our state of mind.

Where you grew up had an impact on your energy field, and in many cases, it still does. In this instance, think of your energy field as your personal space.

If you grew up in a busy city, you probably spent time sharing sidewalks with other city folks. Maybe you were accustomed to riding public transportation, elbow-to-elbow with strangers. You may have double parked when no parking spaces were available, so you waited, or you circled the block a zillion times.

Subsequently, as a city dweller, your energetic field became more compact. Rather than having less energy, it simply means you adjusted your field to avoid intruding on others while protecting your own space.

On the other hand, if you grew up in a rural area, there was more space for your energy field to occupy without bumping up against another person's. Your field naturally expanded outward.

In fact, if you have the opportunity to walk down a sidewalk with only a few people, you can probably guess where a person was raised by how they walk past an oncoming person. You can even do the same thing while networking at a reception.

Pull to mind where were you raised and how much space you prefer around you. Take a moment and think about how you naturally stand when you are chatting with another person.

## FEEL YOUR "EGG"

Since your *Egg* is flexible and flows around your entire body, take the palm of your hand facing outward and gently push outward towards the front. Next, push slowly to each side, then, up above your head and all around. Your *Egg* is strong. It flexes and moves with you.

Even though your *Egg* is sturdy, you might accidentally crack it. If you become angry, or hateful, or frustrated and lash out, your internal hostile energy can literally punch your *Egg* from the inside and cause damage.

However, when you realize you have lashed out, take a moment to forgive yourself. Then, locate any cracks or gaps and smooth them over.

At first, I failed to grasp the concept of repairing my *Egg* and I kept losing my shield. Eventually, I visualized getting shiny duct tape and taping up the cracks. That worked for me.

Over time, I learned faster, more efficient ways to repair my *Egg*. I now do a slight, physical move to smooth over the cracks. By simply waving my hand, my *Egg* is instantly repaired.

You can *Put Your Egg On* and go about your business, just like you would step into a suit of armor. One more time I will remind you to routinely check in for maintenance and smooth out any cracks.

Be sure to put this reminder on your calendar: "Routine Maintenance for my Egg" or simply "Egg"

## WHERE CAN I BUY AN "EGG"?

You can't. *The Egg* is not for sale. You simply visualize your own personal *Egg*. It's free, reusable, and recyclable.

## MY "EGG'S" EVOLUTION

When I first encountered the process, *The Egg* concept sounded dumb to me. I didn't believe it would work, and neither did my husband when I introduced the idea to him.

What I discovered quickly is this: *Believing that any method will work is unnecessary. You just need to continually practice the methods to re-train both your brain and your mind.*

Today, my husband finds putting on his *Egg* especially beneficial before he enters a shopping mall. If he forgets to put on his *Egg*, or he neglects touching base with his *Egg*, he becomes irritable, gets a headache, and can't stand to shop.

## BEING IN THE "EGG"

In the fall of 2015, I spent nine hours in a hospital's ER with my husband, who was experiencing a life-threatening event. Every hour I stood up, took a walk, and drank some water. Nurses and doctors kept asking me why I was so happy.

While driving my husband to the hospital, I had fleeting thoughts about patching any possible cracks and gave thanks for my smooth, intact *Egg*. As I walked about in the ER, rather than consciously thinking about my *Egg*, I was simply *Being in The Egg*.

## DR. MCDREAMY FELT THE EFFECT

My husband had cataract surgery on both eyes early in 2016 along with the installation of a tiny iStent in each eye to relieve the pressure from glaucoma. No, Dr. McDreamy is not the doctor's real name, but he earned it. Combine his refined surgical skill with his winning smile and awesome bedside manner, you have a doctor you probably wished you had in your dreams.

At the follow-up after the second eye surgery, the first thing Dr. McDreamy said touched my heart, "My surgery staff said they felt better having you and your husband around. They felt... well, uplifted."

One of my intentions is to be uplifting during coaching, as well as, with family and friends. I call the concept *energy sharing*. Thank you, Dr. McDreamy, for confirming that positive energy is truly infectious.

## REMOTE INSTALLATION

Both my husband and I were on the road handling magazine marketing and advertising for nearly ten years. In 2005, he was in Oklahoma while I was in California. Mom was at home with our pups in Florida.

During a free day after my meetings, the Weather Channel alert showed a hurricane changing directions, heading directly towards our home on the west coast of Florida. We live only 25 miles from the Gulf of Mexico.

Calling home, I was unable to get through. Frightened, I sat for a moment, settled and asked, "What can I possibly do while 3,000 miles away from home?"

Closing my eyes and focusing on my breathing, the first thought that came to mind was *The Egg*. I had never considered putting on *The Egg* remotely. Even though time and space are relative, the concept was clearly abstract for me.

With that in mind, I went ahead and visually installed *The Egg* around our homestead by including the entire fence bordering our property. While envisioning Mom and the pups safely inside our home, I saw a bright, glowing energy field surrounding our property, which looked a lot like a bubble. I also imagined *The Egg* deflecting gale force winds upwards and away.

On the red-eye flight back to Tampa, I focused on being grateful for Mother's protection, for the safety of our pups, and for all of her gardening stuff. Mother's tools are always scattered everywhere. She works until she's exhausted, drops whatever is in her hand, and comes inside. Keeping her body moving has kept her alive and healthy far longer than the average person.

Landing back in Florida, I was able to reach Mom by phone. She said everything was fine. However, during the ninety-minute drive from the airport, I passed by and saw massive hurricane and tornado damage.

When I entered our subdivision of 103 separate, one-acre lots, chaos was everywhere. Driving up to our home, I was saddened to see every single house and property touching our lot was damaged.

However, I was relieved to discover that our home was completely intact and nothing had even been blown around our acre.

Mom's plastic flower pots were stacked up just where they were when I left. There was a rake leaning against a tree, and beside the tree was a huge pile of leaves.

That was the first time I remotely energetically installed *The Egg*. Using the method that way is now a permanent addition to my toolbox.

## YOUR BODY SPEAKS

You can feel the energy of other people when you are dealing with them in sales, when you're dating, or when you're making love and sexually engaged. At a party, you can sense when someone walks up behind you. Even though no one has physically tapped you on your shoulder, or breathed on your neck, you might feel them, too. Their energy field has overlapped with yours, and you sense them.

When you feel an intruder, you are in jeopardy. Take heed and step back.

If you ever feel the hair stand up on the back of your neck, something just triggered fear. The instinctive part of your brain released chemicals in the fight, flight, or freeze response.

At other times, you feel comfortable when someone enters your energy field. Welcome them.

In another circumstance, you may have goose bumps or shivers that surge through your body in a good way. When the *American Idol* judge, Jennifer Lopez, loved a singer, she often said "You gave me goosies." That singer definitely plucked at J.Lo's heart strings.

Remember, everything is energy. Listen to your body. Your body's energy field is responding to what is going on around you, as well as to your thoughts.

## YOUR BODY IS A SPONGE

It's a fact that we can also absorb energy from other people. Rather than just knowing how others are feeling or what is going on around us, we absorb that energy.

Have you ever seen someone enter a room with a dark cloud hanging over their head? When a person carries tangible, negative energy with them, you feel it. If someone comes in joyful and uplifted, you feel that, too.

To all of that I say, "You must protect your energy field... *literally*, rather than figuratively."

## PREPARE TO GET STARTED

Let me point out that when you deliberately *Put Your Egg On*, you will be using nearly all of your body, softly and gently, but totally. By involving the majority of your body, you occupy your brain and fully engage your mind, body, and spirit to protect your energy.

You will be using your hands, arms, shoulder muscles, neck muscles, and your eyes. To ready your body, you will be using your legs, feet, core muscles, your face, and lungs.

The more you consciously use your body, the more you occupy your brain by *doing a task* rather than continue focusing on whatever is bothering you. The more you rev up your *body-mind connection*, the more positive results you will experience in a shorter time frame.

First, we'll go through a specific process of *locating and feeling your energy field*. Some people are left-brain dominant and want concrete proof. Other people, who are right-brain dominant, are more willing to believe what they visualize.

Please understand. When we clearly visualize, our brain is unable to "know" whether what we "see" in our mind's eye is real or an illusion. On top of that, our thoughts can alter and counteract visioning.

In the '70s, when I was introduced to discovering and truly feeling my own energy field, I wanted tangible evidence. I was clearly left-brain and right-brain driven. Each was codependent on the other looking for answers to satisfy both.

Bouncing back and forth between the brain hemispheres can certainly fracture your mindset and give you one heck of a headache. I've done that more than I'd like to admit.

Trying to locate and feel the outer boundary of my energy field, I kept moving too fast; I was impatient, felt nothing and was frustrated. I kept thinking, "Okay I'm doing that, but I just can't quite feel anything."

Looking back, I believe I was expecting to get a push-back jolt—much like groping under a lamp shade to unscrew a burned-out light bulb, finding no bulb and being zapped. What happens when your fingers inch their way into a turned-on, empty light bulb socket? Ouch!

Or, I was hoping to at least feel strong resistance when I encountered my energy field. Much like you experience when walking across carpet and getting a static electricity snap.

We rarely receive a strong alert. Why? Because our energy field is subtle.

Finally, without consciously knowing what I was doing, I suppose I finally shifted to my right brain. I drew in a slow, deep breath, closed my eyes, exhaled with a sigh, and cleared my mind.

In that moment, I was able to hover my right hand over my left forearm and feel the outer boundary of my energy field. In reality, I had shifted *into* neutral without even knowing the essence of shifting.

Let's begin.

## "PUT YOUR EGG ON" DETAILED STEPS

In the details, you will find a lot of physical movement, some of which may seem odd at first. Do only what is comfortable. If you reach any movement that causes discomfort, remain still. Release the hurt, and envision you are fluidly moving.

**Step 1: Sit comfortably in your chair. Wash and energize your hands.** Feet flat on the floor. Rest your arms by your side, hands in your lap. Look down and notice your hands.

Gently move your hands back and forth as if you're washing them with soap under water. Move one hand over and around the other hand. Luxuriate in the feel of soapy lather.

Finish washing your hands. Rub your palms together fast, back and forth, six times.

**Step 2: Inhale. Exhale with a long sigh and let your right hand hover.** Lift your left elbow and rest your arm in the air in front of your chest, with arm horizontal to the ground. Your left hand is facing down.

Lift your right elbow and arm upward. Open your right hand and slowly move your right palm toward your left arm. Rather than touch your left arm between your wrist and elbow, hover and move your palm over your left forearm to sense your energy field.

**Step 3: Inhale. Close your eyes, exhale with a sigh and "pet" your forearm.** Since we often try to *see and look for* our energy field, move your right hand slightly up and down in the air above your forearm, as if you're gently *petting or stroking* your energy field. When you sense a slight resistance, you have identified your energy field.

Even if you don't feel your energy field directly, you can still sense it; however, if you don't sense it, just imagine that you do.

Release any frustration and acknowledge that your energy field does exist and extends just beyond your skin barrier. Your energy field is there.

**Step 4: Shape your Egg. Eyes still closed.** Imagine an egg surrounding your energy field, encompassing you and free-forming around your body. There is no predefined shape or structure of *The Egg*, and it takes any form or shape you prefer to create. You own it.

Your *Egg* is flexible, rather than brittle like a chicken egg that cracks. Your *Egg* is strong and conforms to your body, like a diving wetsuit.

Fitting loosely and feeling comfortable just to the outside of your energy field, your *Egg* expands as your energy increases. Your *Egg* puts no pressure on your energy while completely protecting you from unwanted energetic assault.

In real time, your *Egg* changes shape and moves with your body, maintaining its protective shield and filter just to the outside of your energy field. *Your Egg fluidly moves WITH you.*

**Step 5: Polish your Egg. Eyes remain closed.** The outside of your *Egg* has a highly-reflective mirrored surface and is any color you prefer. Since your *Egg* is fresh off the assembly line, the surface is brilliant and smooth.

In fact, from positive energy's point of view, the surface is crystal clear and non-existent.

Whenever you check in for maintenance, come back to this point in time. Your *Egg* is now a perfect, intact, smooth, reflective surface that deflects negativity while allowing positivity to pass through.

**Step 6: Now, install your Egg. Inhale, open eyes, smile, and exhale.** Notice and acknowledge that you are taking possession of and installing your *Egg* around your body's energy field.

Turn your head, swivel your body, and look all the way around you. As you move your head, your eyes, shoulders, core and your arms, while balancing your movement with your legs, hips and feet, you engage all your body to openly accept, appreciate and acknowledge your *Egg*.

At this moment, you are installing your *Egg* above your head, behind your back, in front of you and below you... underneath you, under the chair, into the ground or under the floor. Your energy field is now completely encapsulated and surrounded by your *Egg*.

**Step 7: Set your Egg's intention. Inhale. Close your eyes and exhale with a sigh.** See the outside of your *Egg* as a polished, shiny mirrored surface that reflects only negativity and deflects unwanted energy out into the Universe where it becomes neutral and is recycled. If you had reflected that energy back to its source, you might have created bad karma.

Your *Egg* surface is a filter, allowing positivity and nurturing energy to completely reach you. Welcome. Come on in.

One last reminder before we finish... Periodically check your *Egg* for cracks and repair. Consider putting reminders on your calendar.

Open your eyes and smile. You are now fully protected.

## "PUT YOUR EGG ON" AT-A-GLANCE

1. **Sit comfortably. Wash and energize your hands.** Rub palms together fast, six times.

2. **Breathe and let your right hand hover over your left arm.** Feel your energy field.

3. **Close your eyes. Gently "pet" your left forearm.** Sense a slight resistance.

4. **Shape your Egg.** Imagine your *Egg* as it free-forms around your body. Your *Egg* is flexible, strong and fluid.

5. **Polish your Egg's highly-reflective mirrored surface.** Eyes remain closed.

6. **Install your Egg.** Open eyes, smile and take possession of your *Egg* by involving your entire body as you look all the way around you.

7. **Set your Egg's intention.** Close your eyes and see your *Egg's* shiny mirrored surface deflecting only negative energy while welcoming pure positivity.

**Maintenance:** Rather than initially *Putting Your Egg On* quickly or skimming, please own the process outlined in the previous Details section. The At-A-Glance above is a reminder of those seven steps. Locate and acknowledge your energy field and intentionally install your *Egg*.

Consider using the *Egg's* QuickShift™ that follows as your guide to regularly check-in for maintenance. In two deep breaths coupled with deliberate movement, you can locate and intentionally smooth over *Egg* fractures while energizing self. By including body engagement, you mind, body, and spirit can become totally involved and shifted away from emotional strife. Once there, you easily repair.

## "THE EGG" MAINTENANCE QUICKSHIFT™

1. **Close your eyes. Take one slow, deep breath in and out as you detach. Physically move your head and body as you look about.** Inside your mind's eye, look around and notice any *Egg* cracks or fractures.

2. **As you inhale deeply again, slowly move hands from below your waist, up your core to the sky.** Palms facing inward and upward collecting energy. Move hands up along center, up past your chest. Turn your palms upward to the sky as arms fully extend. Hands fully charged.

3. **As you exhale with palms facing outward, slowly sweep your hands downward in a full arc to your side.** Send healing energy from your hands to your *Egg*, totally sealing any cracks, fractures or holes.

## PROGRESS CONFIRMATION

Since you have now experienced your eighth MindShift Exercise™ *Put Your Egg On*, I suggest you intentionally say the following aloud:

> *"I am taking control of my mind and creating the life I want, now that I have put on my flexible, mirrored Egg, which completely surrounds my energy field, deflects negativity, while allowing positive energy to flow through to me."*

## UP NEXT...

In the next chapter, you'll discover another effective way to fuel up, change your focus, and recharge your batteries. This method is a full, physical body engagement called *Pit Stop*. You may be surprised to learn that your pit crew is near at hand.

Once again, if you are physically impaired and unable to move parts of your body, or if you prefer to remain still for whatever reason, you can still engage your physical body by envisioning you are, indeed, moving. Our brain is unable to know the difference.

Now, go and discover where to find your pit crew.

# CHAPTER 13
## PIT STOP (MSE 9)

Now that you're cruising along and have discovered easy ways to shift your mindset, your ninth MindShift Exercise™ is *Pit Stop*. Mentally checking in to support and maintain your energy is vital. However, sometimes I unconsciously set that aside.

What I knew I needed was a fast way to refuel, change my focus, and recharge my batteries. Otherwise, I seemed to spin my wheels and get bogged down in the mud.

Imagine what happens when a race car driver pulls in for a full-blown pit stop. The driver's pit crew services the car in a flash. They can change all four tires, *power-add* a full tank of fuel, while wiping the grill and making minor adjustments to the vehicle.

**Question:** How long does it take for an expert, six-person team to finish a complete pit stop during a race?

**Answer:** Here we need a drum roll. The answer is twelve seconds!

Since we normally blink our eyes once about every four seconds, a well-formed pit crew can do a full pit stop in about three eye blinks! What possible strategy did the team use to accomplish all that lightning fast?

Here's the key: At the core, the crew members fully practice their skills as a team so they can act in harmony. Then, in real time, the crew chief orchestrates and shifts the team's strategy based on the race length, caution flags, fuel mileage, and tire wear.

On a personal level, we can factor in life changes to create our own strategy for fluid MindShifting. First, look at the big picture—your life's road map—then, ask yourself, "What is happening right now?"

With that framework in mind, sort through your *MindShift Toolbox*™ and create your personal *MindShift Tool Belt*™. You decide which methods to use and when; but you must first practice, learn and customize your tool belt to fit you. You are your own crew chief.

## WHERE IS MY PIT CREW?

Look at your hands. You have your very own, built-in, pit crew at your fingertips—IN YOUR HANDS. We have more connections *in the palm of our hands to our brain* than any other body part, men and women alike. Our hands do more different things than any other part of our body.

Rather than focusing on our thoughts, or how to think a particular way, this method is a full, physical-body engagement. *Pit Stop* has become a centering technique that is, by itself, powerful.

In reality, *Pit Stop* is a standalone MindShift Exercise™. Of course, you can use this *full-body-process* along with any other method; your choice because you are the boss.

174

## ROUTINE MAINTENANCE

How often do you put fuel into your motorized vehicle or plug in your hybrid car? Do you wait until the fuel gauge nears empty, or do you disregard the gauge altogether until the low-fuel light flashes on your dashboard? You know exactly what happens when your vehicle runs out of fuel.

The engine sputters and stops. You coast to the side of the road. Worst yet, your vehicle stops in the middle of a busy highway, directly in the path of oncoming traffic.

Think about how often you check your oil and when you have the oil changed. Have you put "oil change" on your calendar? Despite my bull-headed stubbornness, I finally added "oil change" to our over-sized calendar in the kitchen.

Do you like to wait while the oil is being changed, or do you feel it is a waste of your time? Actually, I now enjoy waiting during an oil change at my favorite place. When I drive up, they greet me with a smile and call me by my name. While waiting for the oil change, I take a bit of me-time in their comfortable waiting room.

Consider when you had your radiator flushed, or when your transmission fluid was changed. I read a blog post on *Popular Mechanics* about transmission fluid and kept thinking the writer had been reading my MindShifting journal:

> *"You drive the same route to work every day—same open stretches, same intersections and same stop-and-go. But today there's a subtle discord in the usual harmony, a blip on your vehicle radar, a bad vibe in your mechanical karma.*
>
> *Your vehicle [seemed to] oddly shift... late and soft [not as smoothly as it should be shifting]. Later when you pull into the driveway, you sense something peculiar. Letting your car idle, you pull the dipstick out of your auto transmission.*

*Fresh automatic transmission fluid is bright red and has a distinct petroleum smell. Your dipstick shows a low level, is the color of institutional linoleum, and smells like the bottom of a barbecue pit after a biker wedding. Your transmission fluid is badly in need of changing and the tranny may already be damaged."*

Too often, we put off maintaining our vehicles until our vehicle tells us, "You waited too long!" Once again from firsthand experience, I know that fact is true. I've learned harsh and expensive lessons from failing to do routine maintenance on our cars, as well as, neglecting to maintain my own human, body vehicle.

## WAITING HURTS

We have a 6-foot 5-inch friend, a brother-from-different-parents, who helps Mama Peggy in her garden several days a week. He surprised us by asking to borrow Mom's Volkswagen. He looks funny driving the VW, as do I.

"Of course, you can borrow the car," we said. "What happened?"

He explained. Immediately after filling his tank, his truck crawled along and just won't pick up speed. He dropped his truck off at his mechanic near our home. The mechanic did one test drive after another and was unable to replicate the truck's continual crawl, however, the truck repeatedly went from crawling to lurching forward.

When asked, our friend said he always waited to refuel until his tank was nearly empty. It appears he had damaged his truck by waiting too long. His truck gave him notice by rebelling like a hormonal teenager.

Waiting to refuel until the vehicle nears empty can cause damage. Over time, sludge builds up in the fuel tank and settles to the bottom. When the fuel level gets too low, the gunk can be sucked up into the system.

The same thing happens with our physical body. Putting off taking care of our body and our mind can seriously damage or destroy our life. When I waited to take care of me and focused on just caring for others, my body broke.

This morning before I started wrapping up this chapter, I sat down for a quick mental snack. My cozy office is lined with all sorts of thought-provoking objects. I keep a book beside my recliner, which sits to the right of my desk.

Sometimes, I read a bit. Other times, I practice an existing MindShifting method, re-frame that particular one or shift through possible steps for a new one. Each time, I ponder and chew awhile. The following jumped off the page from an angel book by Doreen Virtue about valuing yourself:

> "It's impossible to separate what you do to yourself and what you do for others—it's like trying to nurture and feed only certain leaves on a tree! That's impossible, of course, but it's exactly what you're trying to do when you attempt to put yourself last."

That's right. You must come first. Routine maintenance can help you shore up your energy, repair leaks, and shift your mindset.

Just as our bodies need both rest and nourishment, so do our minds. We need to feed, rest, and exercise both our mental muscles and our body.

## ADD REMINDERS

In order to learn how to shift your mindset smoothly, integrate MindShifting into the routine maintenance for your life-body-vehicle. You can easily turn MindShifting into a habit by simply remembering to remember. In fact, my husband and I still put "date night" on our calendars and joyfully comply.

My reminder is "MT" for me-time. You might create an icon or image that is easy to draw as a fun reminder on your kitchen calendar or in your planner. To remind us to put the liquid medicine on our pups to protect them from heart worm, fleas, and ticks, I draw a puppy paw print on the calendar with a sharp red marker.

Schedule your *Pit Stop* so you take more time for you. Use whatever tool works for you.

- Put reminders on your kitchen calendar throughout the year.
- Write reminders in your datebook or planner.
- Set reminders on your computer and smart phones.
- Add reminders to your internal calendar.
- Give permission to your spouse or partner, allowing them to remind you to take a break to recharge your body and your mind.

There are also reminder apps you can install on your mobile device. Pick one that resonates with you. I use one with a multiple-overlapping-calendar feature that helps me decide priorities. Otherwise, juggling the available time in my life is dangerous, especially when I continually bounce around from self-care, to caregiving, coaching, speaking, writing, consulting, traveling, playing, and competing.

Calendaring helps me decide where to focus; otherwise, I allow mindset demons to intrude and pull me all over the place. Physically *trying* to do this, then that, and maybe that other thing, prevents me from focusing and completing even one simple step. That may sound familiar to you, too.

Let's begin.

## "PIT STOP" OVERVIEW

**Intention:** To balance, repair and energize your physical wellbeing by fully engaging your mind, body, and spirit.

**How:** Even though this method might appear complex at first, it is very simple. However, detailed written explanations always make simple steps appear complicated. In reality, *Pit Stop* can take as little as 90 seconds to do and is a great way to start your day. I've made it a habit to spend a bit longer luxuriating in the process by polishing my *Egg* first thing in the morning.

To illustrate the simplicity of this technique, I've included a short video with your bonus package where I personally show you the movements. Be sure to grab your pack on my personal site: **www.DonnaBlevins.com/mindshift**

The physicality of this method also blends my experience with the practices of Tai Chi, a gentle way to fight stress, as well as QiGong (chee-gong). In essence, Tai Chi and QiGong are low-impact, moving meditations.

I'm going to ask you to perform some physical movements. *Taking action, rather than just trying to think positive thoughts, is the root of all MindShift Exercises*™. I've often thought of this form as "magnetized glue" that helps pull fragmented parts back together, and then anchors them in place.

When? Using this method can help you prepare to get back to work, finish a project, go into a meeting, start a new endeavor, refocus, or even go to sleep.

Physically moving particular ways can help you stop worrying and stressing while opening up and harmonizing your energetic fields. At the same time, these types of gentle movements recharge your batteries directly, instead of burning fuel and leaving you initially feeling tired like many physical workouts do.

The original title for this MindShifting exercise was *"Hug. Polish. Give Thanks."* That title says a lot about how *Pit Stop* works. The process activates your mind-body-spirit connection by *hugging, polishing, and giving thanks*, while balancing your male and female energies and harmonizing your entire body.

## "PIT STOP" DETAILED STEPS

Start and end with a long drink of water. With your eyes closed, allow your hands to touch, move, and remain in contact with your body. Your hands will vacuum up and then flick away any residual effects of negativity you've been holding onto. Move through the exercise with gratitude, imagining you are spit-shining your energetic field.

The power is in the palm of your hands. As you move your hands, notice the sensations while your hands polish and bring shining light to your body.

Notice how your body feels being touched, how your entire body begins to glow, how your body straightens and becomes stronger.

Let's begin.

### Step 1: Position yourself seated. Have a glass of cool water by your side.

Sit up straight in your chair, comfortable and relaxed. Plant both of your feet flat on the floor, directly under your knees and hip-width apart, connected to Mother Earth.

Take a long, cool drink of water. Drinking the water starts the process.

Close your eyes. As you slowly breathe in, fill your lungs with bright, light rays from Father Sun.

Exhale and let go of darkness. Allow your shoulders to comfortably drop as you settle into your calm space.

**Step 2: Balance your left side, release tension and energize.**

Right hand to left shoulder: Rotate your hand slowly in circular motions around your left shoulder three times.

Stroke your hand down your left arm to your wrist. At the bottom of the stroke, allow the palm and fingers of your right hand to caress and massage your left hand. Move your right hand over and around your left hand, as your left hand remains at rest, receives the love, and balances. Then, stroke all the way back up to your shoulder. Repeat three times.

**Step 3: Balance your right side, release tension and energize.**

Left hand to right shoulder: Rotate your hand slowly in circular motions around your right shoulder three times.

Stroke your hand down your right arm to your wrist. At the bottom of the stroke, allow the palm and fingers of your left hand to massage and caress your right hand, as your right hand remains at rest, receives love, and balances. Then, stroke all the way back up to your shoulder. Repeat three times.

**Step 4: Hug yourself and appreciate who you are. Engage and balance your entire body. Further energize. Light your fire!**

Notice how straight you are sitting in your chair, with your back away from the back of the chair. Rather than leaning back, your upper torso is freely at ease.

Cross your arms, and hug yourself. Take a few moments and continue hugging, swaying gently from side to side, smiling and reveling in who you are. Acknowledge and appreciate you—for you are worthy just the way you are. Slowly breathe in and out in unison as you sway.

Your head moves too. Rather than holding your head still and locked in place, or forcing your head to move a particular way, allow your head to gently move in concert with swaying. Only do what is comfortable.

Engage the rest of your body. As you rock from side to side, balance your movements by engaging the other side of your body. When you sway to the left, push slightly down with your right foot and engage your right calf, thigh, and butt muscles. When you sway to the right, activate the left side.

Now energize. Light your fire just as a scout lights a fire without a match and sparks the flame. With your hands on your biceps, move your hands quickly from elbow to shoulder six times, as if you are cold and warming yourself. You are now glowing and getting warmer.

**Step 5: Remain intentional and keenly aware. Inhale, stroke diagonally, exhale, flick.**

Inhale deeply as you stroke your hands diagonally across your body. At the end of the motion, exhale forcefully as you flick your fingers sharply—as if you are flipping electrostatic lint off your fingertips.

From the hugging position with your arms crossed, breathe in deeply as you draw your hands across your chest, downward toward your hips and out to the sides. While stroking your fingertips lightly across your chest, intentionally attract and collect any residue of negative energy.

Pull your hands to both sides away from your body. Forcefully exhale through pursed lips and aggressively flick away the darkness.

Repeat two more times. Inhale fully; stroke diagonally and down across your chest. Exhale loudly and flick away.

As you slowly inhale and draw your fingers across your body, intentionally see your hands become the vacuum cleaner that sucks the negativity out of both your body and your mind.

Further hold your awareness at its peak. Loudly exhale as you forcefully flick your fingers. As you do so, you release the crap you've been holding onto, which has been sapping your energy and continually distracting you.

**Step 6: Bow your head and give thanks for your energetic renewal.**

Slowly inhale and exhale as you smile and bring both hands to your face. Touch your forehead with all your fingers. Rest your thumbs on your jaw line or cheeks, whichever is most natural for you.

As you inhale, breathe in a final, bright-white-light booster. As you exhale, slowly drop your shoulders and completely release any remaining stress.

Give thanks for being the crew chief and fully engaging your own, built-in pit crew, which is at your fingertips—IN YOUR HANDS. You have now released negative residue, centered yourself, and power-added fuel.

See your body balanced, polished, glowing, and energetically re-charged.

**Step 7: Open your eyes and take a long, cool drink of water. You are now connected, polished, smoothed, revitalized, balanced and ready to go. Drinking the water has sealed the process.**

Open your internal calendar and add these simple *body-polishing steps* to your daily routine. Or, at the very least, use this method as your go-to-process when you notice you are energetically fractured, or you simply want to raise your own energy.

Remember, your pit crew is in the palm of your hands, and you are the crew chief.

## "PIT STOP" AT-A-GLANCE

1. **Sit up straight, relaxed, feet flat on floor connecting to Mother Earth.** Take a long, cool drink of water to start the process. Close eyes. Breathe in light rays from Father Sun. Exhale darkness. Drop shoulders, settle into calm.

2. **Balance your left side, release tension and energize. Right hand to left shoulder.** Rotate hand around shoulder three times. Move hand from shoulder to wrist/hand three times. At the bottom of each stroke, caress and balance your left hand, as your left hand remains receptive.

3. **Balance your right side, release tension and energize. Left hand to right shoulder.** Rotate hand around shoulder three times. Move hand from shoulder to wrist/hand three times. At the bottom of the stroke, caress and balance your right hand, as your right hand remains receptive.

4. **Hug yourself and appreciate who you are. Engage and balance your entire body. Further energize. Light your fire!** Sit upright, rather than leaning back in your chair. Cross arms and hug yourself. Gently sway from side to side, smiling and reveling in who you are. Softly move your head in concert with swaying. Engage your entire body by counterbalancing your sway with the opposite side of your body—from your foot all the way to your butt. Briskly rub your arms from elbow to shoulder six times to warm yourself.

5. **From hugging position, stroke diagonally across body and flick negative residue.** With fingertips touching body, inhale deeply and draw hands across chest... downward towards hips and to the side. Exhale forcefully as you flick your fingers sharply, releasing negative residue. Repeat twice more, remaining intentional with heightened awareness.

6. **Bow your head and give thanks for your energetic renewal.** Inhale and exhale slowly. Smile and bring hands to face. Touch forehead with fingers and rest thumbs on face. Breathe in a bright-white-light booster. Breathe out. Release remaining stress and drop your shoulders. See your body polished, glowing, and energetically re-charged.

7. **Open eyes. Take a long, cool drink of water that seals the process.** You are now polished, smoothed, revitalized, and ready to go.

**Want an even faster Pit Stop?** You might have blown a gasket... or, almost made a stupid mistake and lashed out... or, just moments before stepping into a vital meeting, your shoulders were pulled up so tight against your ears, you had no neck. I know I've done that and been there, too.

When any of these types of crucial moments occur, you need a way to physically engage your mind-body shift right on the spot and disconnect completely from fueling fear, anger, stupidity, and amplifying stress. Simply put, you need to immediately shake it off. And, you can.

Once you have practiced the *Pit Stop* routine until it becomes natural, you can effectively do a modified QuickShift™ version using steps four and five from the Detailed Steps. You'll find "shaking your hands" added within the QuickShift™. I recommend adding forgiveness at the beginning, which belongs as the engagement step in many of the MindShift Exercises™.

## "PIT STOP" QUICKSHIFT™

Step away to a private place or just out of sight. Of course, you can visualize this process within your mind's eye; however, when you are physically able to move, take action and fully activate your body-mind connection.

1. **Forgive yourself.** Take a slow, deep forgiving breath, and as you exhale, release the guilt.

2. **Hug yourself and appreciate who you are. Light your fire!** Gently sway from side to side, smiling and giving thanks for who you are. Briskly rub your arms six times.

3. **Stroke diagonally across body, flick negative residue and shake your hands.** Inhale deeply and draw fingertips across chest and downward to the side. Exhale forcefully. Flick your fingers sharply, releasing negative residue. Shake your hands vigorously, as if you are shaking water off your hands.

**Faster Yet?** Step out of sight for a brief moment. Flick your fingers and shake your hands while rotating your shoulders.

## PROGRESS CONFIRMATION

Since you have experienced your ninth MindShift Exercise™ *Pit Stop*, I suggest you intentionally say the following aloud:

> "I am taking full control of my mind and loving who I
> am, now that I come first and faithfully take me-time
> for a Pit Stop; using the power in the palm of my
> hands, I body-polish to repair and energize, hug myself
> and give thanks."

## UP NEXT...

In the next chapter, you will discover that we do have the innate ability to let go of the mental trash that keeps polluting our life. Rather than having to wait for garbage day, you can *Toss Out the Trash* with a fast mental shift coupled with another flick of the wrist.

Read on. Many people have told me that they simply love the process.

# CHAPTER 14
## TOSS THE TRASH (MSE 10)

During mastermind conference calls with other authors, I'm usually a fly-on-the-wall and learn by listening. However, during one session, the leader asked me to share one of my techniques. I chose *Toss Out the Trash,* which is going to be your tenth MindShift Exercise™.

The response was heartwarming. There were ripples of laughter along with, "Yes, I'm going to use THAT EVERY DAY!"

The following day, I posted a question in our private Facebook group about whether another MindShifting method also belonged in this book. The leader of the group said, "I can't say with 100% surety about the other, since I have not heard or seen it yet, but *Toss Out the Trash* should be there, for sure! And, use the vivid imagery you used on the call with us."

## PITY PARTY

As a child, when I chattered on and on about how I had screwed up, Mama Peggy often said, "Stop having a pity party. Think a bit. Learn. Then, just let it go."

Carrying lessons forward, I now open my coaching sessions by saying, *"I'm creating a safe place for you that is guilt-free, blame-free, judgment-free, and yes, whine-free. Just leave the whining at the door."*

When we look at whatever has happened in a self-hating way, we often start with, "Why am I always wrong?" Our focus then becomes, "It's me! I am the problem."

Instantly slipping into the self-judgmental mode allows *the thing* to bully us, control our emotions, and disrupt our life. In contrast, detached interest creates a safe environment where we can look at our mistakes, troubles, and challenges while we glean life lessons.

> **Key Point: *Detaching is productive and healthy. However, disregarding is entirely different and can be harmful.***

When we completely ignore our mental trash, we create a compost pile of garbage in our mind. When we neglect safely processing our mistakes and challenges, we dig a hole and bury the source deep in our subconscious, effectively creating fertilizer.

We become stressed. We are no longer calm (*at ease*) and essentially feed our illness (*dis-ease*); we provide food, a place to eat, grow, and create more of the same. Toxic mental garbage can literally make us physically sick.

Rummaging through our head trash, then taking time to reflect before taking the trash to the curb, clearly gives us perspective and contrast. The process of detached reflection of "life's by-product" can be life-changing.

For me, once I've chewed on it for a while, tossing out the trash is simply uplifting. The positive side effect of letting go nurtures our mind and can transform into self-healing superpowers. Yet, in my opinion, I believe tossing mental trash early and often is preferred. The habit helps maintain wellness.

## GARBAGE COLLECTOR UNIFORM

Much of my mental garbage stinks and behaves like emotionally, radioactive slime. Before dragging up situations from my life's timeline, I imagine stepping into full protection... kind of like wearing a "mental hazmat suit" to prevent spawning more traumas.

Mentally touching much of my past without safeguards often gives me the shudders. My mindset fractures and allows less-than worthless thoughts to surface.

In my mind's eye, rather than simply putting on my detached-observer hat, I upgrade and put on full-body protection. The suit comes equipped with a helmet and respirator.

When I take the plunge and dredge up the residue from my past mistakes, I look like a deep sea welder. Hmm... that sounds like another MindShift Exercise™ exists within that thought.

Some of my garbage still manages to hide and ferment. I continue to sort through head trash and release as I gracefully age. It has taken me decades to embrace the aging-gracefully concept; yet the older I get, the deeper I fall in love with me.

The only way I became "the me" that I am, was for me to have chosen my path. There's still a part of me that says, *"Yes, BUUUUTT... YOU didn't choose that... or that... or that!"*

Yes, I did. I chose when to take the wheel and when to remain the unwitting passenger.

Take a few moments and consider where you are right now and what your head trash looks like. I suggest you discard your self-judgmental attitude, and at the very least, don your detached-observer hat. You might want to create your own garbage disposal gear.

## RECORDING BECAME MY DETACHED OBSERVER

When I first wanted to become a speaker forty-five years ago, a wise man told me, "Always record yourself. Regardless of where you talk, ALWAYS record yourself. That way you can listen back, keep what you want, and trash what you don't."

Recording became my concealed weapon. Words have power, and I wanted to discover who I was by listening to replays of me speaking. Recordings helped me toss the trash, keep the gems, and polish the diamonds hiding just below the surface.

In those days, investment in the highest quality, small electronic equipment was awfully expensive—more than most people would earn in a month. Despite the cost, I never hesitated. I fully committed, and the payoff for me over the years has been groundbreaking.

Listening to recordings of what I had previously said gives me a way to *chew on it for a while.* The process also became my built-in accountability partner where I talk with myself in a productive way: *"What sounds good? What might I leave out? Okay. Keep this. No, trash that. Refine here a bit more."*

LIVE audience recordings have also given me an unexpected way to unearth exactly what the listeners like. Listening to a recording and hearing laughter cascade through the audience, I get excited. The message came through, *"You made them happy! They want more of that!"*

As a towering, outspoken young adult, I envisioned myself as a stand-up comic, standing out in the crowd and being noticed because of my height. Today, my intention of adding laughter-medicine inside my message is entirely different.

Laughter is healthy for our body, mind, and spirit. In fact, I believe laughter can help dislodge head trash and begin to dissolve sticky remnants.

The body's natural, feel-good chemicals are released in response to laughing. This veritable happy, feel-good cocktail includes endorphins (pain killers), oxytocin (empathy hormone), and dopamine (happy hormone, also released during smiling). Simultaneously, laughter becomes a triggering emotion that can anchor a fun, positive, uplifting experience in our conscious and subconscious mind.

The result? By anchoring uplifting content with smiles and laughter, we can pull up highly-charged positive memories, or have gleeful flashbacks, which raise our energy frequency rather than access terrifying memories that pull us down.

## SIFTING THROUGH GARBAGE

In this moment, I'd like to re-frame PTSD from "Post-Traumatic Stress Disorder" to "Positively Terrific Satisfying Distraction." To me that sounds like laughter.

Distracting our mind by laughing satisfies our soul, feels terrific, and plants positive seeds in our subconscious mind. The cause of negative PTSD is the onslaught of highly-charged emotions as a result of "witnessing traumatic or life-threatening events."

After serving as a "Tunnel Rat" in Vietnam, my husband developed deep-seated, terrifying PTSD which he refuses to pull out and dump. His shrink said, "Sometimes it's best to leave the worst buried deep and ignore it."

At least, that's what my husband said his psychiatrist suggested. I bet that is my husband's version of something the doc said, rather than what the shrink actually meant.

February 2016 was the 50th anniversary of my husband starting his first of two tours in Vietnam. At the beginning of March, he began dealing with sleepless nights again. He finally admitted he was having flashbacks that kept him awake.

His temper flared. He became critical and judgmental, which is the complete opposite of his natural personality.

In my quest to locate a solution to my husband's dark PTSD, I embraced shifting his mindset with laughter. When he looks up with a scowl as I walk into the room, I now understand his reaction comes from his inside residue and has nothing to do with me. With that realization, I have started doing silly things to distract him and help him shift to a positive, satisfying moment.

Round, melon breasts run in my family, but I had none until I blossomed at the age of 30. Today, when I yank off my top and hop around the room, my husband's frown instantly turns upside down.

That's my way of transforming PTSD into "Positively Terrific Satisfying Distraction." Feel free to let your imagination run with that. Hopefully, I put a smile on your face, too.

When anything I say or write causes the ripple effect of *Hmm'ing*, chuckling, or laughing, I trust that adds more value to what I bring to this world. Hopefully in this book, you have chuckled and smiled more than once. While I write and share my stories, I think playing with words is healthy for me as well.

## "TOSS OUT THE TRASH" OVERVIEW

**Intention:** To de-stress your body and de-clutter your mind by tossing out your head trash rather than allowing garbage to ferment and sour deep inside your subconscious mind.

**When to Use:** Mind clutter keeps pulling you this way, then that way. You fret and worry. You lay awake focusing on what desperately bothers you. Your thoughts go from bad to worse.

The Details section below is a portion of a recorded group coaching session, which was the first time I officially shared *Toss Out the Trash* with my clients. Previously, I had been saying, "Just toss out your head trash," and they wanted to know exactly how.

This method uses a different way of fast breathing that I find empowering. My first exposure to fast breathing was when I became a certified instructor for QiGong (*chee-gong*) in 2015. I was amazed that breathing this way cleared my head and invigorated my body rather than leaving me dizzy and light-headed.

## IS FAST BREATHING REQUIRED?

No. You choose. Consider these facts:

- Inhaling and exhaling deeply and equally is healthy for our body while clearly shifting our mind away from worry, fret, and fear. Equally breathing in and out also balances our carbon dioxide and oxygen exchange.

- Breathing fast, equal and deep, requires our brain and body to pay attention to what we are doing. There is no autopilot for fast breathing.

- Deep, fast breathing is entirely different from shallow, rapid breathing, which is harmful. Shallow, rapid breathing reduces the oxygen in the blood and might result from (or even create) anxiety, as well as any number of physical ailments.

After I began to experience the power of breathing through both Tai Chi and QiGong, I added fast breathing while mentally stepping up the stairs. In fact, I use "fast-breathe-in-deep" coupled with "fast-breathe-out-complete" all by itself.

My intention of adding fast breathing to MindShifting gives you another way to energize and move to the moment. Rather than replacing slow, conscious inhaling while exhaling through gently pursed lips, fast breathing adds a different dimension. Both belong in your MindShift Toolbox™, ready for your immediate access.

## "TOSS OUT THE TRASH" DETAILED STEPS

The following is a portion of the transcript during a group coaching session:

We have all experienced worry or "mad frets," as I call them. When we re-live mistakes, we fret about guilt, or judgment, or blame. There's one good term for all that, which is "Head Trash!" That's what we're going to do today... *Toss Out the Trash!*

Tossing your mental trash is easy and more fun than you might expect. The long version uses controlled, fast breathing, which is very different than the controlled, slow way we usually breathe during MindShifting—*in, slowly and deep through your nose; out, slowly and complete through pursed lips.*

**Let me explain balancing fast breathing.** You will forcefully breathe in and out fast, but not shallow. Breathe using your diaphragm by moving abdominal and chest muscles together—*pulling breath in, fast and deep; then, pushing breath out, fast and complete.* Equal amounts of air, both in and out.

With your eyes closed, you will visualize walking up steps, slowly and intentionally, while you fast breathe and pause with each step. If you're driving, find a safe place to park. Start by putting your feet flat on the floor and sit up straight. You will be using your diaphragm, chest, and stomach muscles to fast breathe.

**Step 1: Now that you are sitting in a safe place, let's begin.**

Imagine that you've just arrived home, and your envisioned home has two stories. Walk up three steps to your front porch. Go through the front door, walk a few steps forward and turn to your right.

Before you climb the steps to the second floor, let me talk you through the process first. In a moment, you will travel up seven steps to the landing, fully conscious of each step.

Then, you will turn to your left and walk up seven more steps to the second floor. As long as this is comfortable for you while mentally walking up the steps, you will fast breathe with each step.

**Step 2: Walk up the steps.** As you step up to each step, you will breathe in. Then, as you pause and bring your other foot up to the next step, you will breathe out.

Because of my completely fused ankle, as I walk up the stairs in real life, I intentionally step up with the same foot each time. Then, I pause as I bring the other foot up to that step's tread. In reality, that brief moment of intentionally stepping has become a personal meditation-in-motion for me.

Fortunately, in my mind's eye, both ankles move smoothly as I alternate feet with each step. Sometimes, as I envision the steps, rather than plant both feet on a tread, I pause with the foot I'm moving and balance in the air, knee pulled up... much like you might have seen in the *Karate Kid* movie where Daniel balances on one foot just before he does the Crane Kick.

Okay. Now step-by-step with me. Remember to use your chest, stomach and diaphragm muscles to fast breathe in and out with each step.

Step up 1, breathe in a quick, deep breath. Pause; quick, full breath out.

Step up 2, breathe in quick and deep. Pause; quick, full breath out.

Step up 3, breathe in quick. Pause; quick breath out.

Step up 4, in quick. Pause; out quick.

Step up 5, in quick. Pause; out quick.

Step up 6, in quick. Pause; out quick.

Step up 7, in quick. Pause; out quick.

Turn to the left on the landing, and you will go up seven more steps to the 2nd floor. Continue fast breathing. Step up and breathe in a quick, deep breath. Pause, quick full breath out and complete.

Step 1, breathe in; pause, breathe out.

Step 2, breathe in; pause, breathe out.

Step 3, breathe in; pause, breathe out.

Step 4, breathe in; pause, breathe out.

Step 5, breathe in; pause, breathe out.

Step 6, breathe in; pause, breathe out.

Step 7, breathe in; pause, breathe out.

**Step 3: Now, you are on the second floor. Walk down the hallway and take the first door on the right.** I want you to mentally build the room in your own home. This room will become perfectly yours where you can come in a moment's notice and toss your trash.

When you walk into the room, look around. The room is clean and bare, free of clutter and noise. There is no furniture in the room. The room is filled with peace and quiet. The walls and ceiling are painted a soft, neutral shade… white, gray, pastel… whatever color you envision.

The polished, wooden floor grounds you. For me, the floor is light oak. You choose the wood. It is now your room.

The room is perfect. Void of any baggage, the room is a quiet place where you can find peace.

**Step 4: At the far end of the room is a wide-open window, with garbage bags hung on the wall to the right.** Walk over to the window and notice there is something to the right of the window. Move closer. You see a massive roll of garbage bags mounted to the wall at the perfect height for you. Bags are always there, and the roll is always full.

**Step 5: Reach over and grab a garbage bag.** Now is the perfect time to collect your trash. Open up the garbage bag and think about the things that have been chewing at your mind.

Reach into your head with your hand. Pull out those less-than, worrisome words and thoughts that are self-defeating, and put them in this garbage bag. Whatever they are, they go into the bag.

Gently shake your head. Your mental trash flows out of your head, much like dry salt coming out of a salt shaker. Everything will tumble directly into this bag.

Tie the bag. The big window is wide open directly in front of you.

**Step 6: Pitch it. Toss it.**

Like a baseball pitcher, pull your arm back all the way and toss the bag out the window. The bag simply vaporizes and transforms into pure, neutral energy. The full bag is gone. No longer trash. No longer there. Your head trash is neutralized and recycled.

**Step 7: Open your eyes now. Sit there breathing in and out slowly.** Notice how calm you feel.

**Step 8: More trash?** Whenever you want to return, you can instantly come back to your *de-stress trash room*. If you wake up in the middle of the night and something is chewing at you, in the blink of an eye you can come back to this room. You can then pull off a garbage bag and put those stressful thoughts, feelings, fears, and emotions into the bag and toss it. All that crap will be gone!

When mental trash crops back up again, you can instantly come back to the room and toss it again. The more often you de-trash the less frequently you will need to.

There is an unlimited and ever-abundant supply of garbage bags. This is a magical, powerful room.

*(Opened up the call on the recorded conference line.)*

> *Donna: How did Toss Out the Trash work for you?*
>
> *Client: After having a stressful day, this worked out great for me. I got up at 5 a.m., had sales meetings all day and just walked in the door a few minutes before we started. I felt stressed when we started. Now I am relaxed!*
>
> *Donna: Can you see how you can use this method regularly?*
>
> *Client: Oh, absolutely! To get rid of a lot of worries. Sometimes in the middle of the night I can't sleep. It will be a great thing to do.*

End of Transcript

## TRASH ROOM BUILDER

The first time I experienced a formal, guided mediation, I came across my seemingly magical trash room. Time literally flew for me. I felt like it took me about three minutes to find and experience this room. In reality, the guided mediation took nearly an hour.

Rather than mentioning anything about throwing out mental trash, our instruction was, "Open the door and walk in. You will find whatever you need."

I guess that was what my mind told me, *"It's time to dump your head trash!"* This room has been with me for more than thirty years. Over time, I added fast breathing.

## "TOSS OUT THE TRASH" AT-A-GLANCE

1. **Sit comfortably and close your eyes. You've arrived home to your imagined two-story house.** Walk up three steps to front porch, through the front door, a few steps forward and turn to your right. You are at the foot of the stairway to the second floor.

2. **Tie each breath to a step. With each step up, quick breath in; pause; then quick breath out completely.** Step up first flight, 7 steps to the landing. Turn to your left. Continue on for 7 more steps to the second floor.

3. **On the second floor, walk down the hallway and into the first door on the right, which is your "de-stress" room.** Look around. There is no furniture. The walls are neutral, and the wooden floor grounds you. The room is spotless, peaceful and quiet.

4. **Walk over to the wide-open window at the far end of the room. Garbage bags hang on the wall to the right.** The

unlimited, ever-abundant roll of garbage bags is at the perfect height for you.

5. **Reach over and grab a garbage bag.** Open up the bag and think about the things that are mentally chewing at you...the troubles, worries, and emotional stress, whatever. Drop any mental trash that comes to mind into the garbage bag. Tie up the bag.

6. **Like a baseball pitcher, pull your arm back all the way and toss the bag out the window.** The bag vaporizes and transforms into pure, neutralized energy. That head trash vanishes.

7. **Open your eyes; breathe in and out slowly.** You are now calm and at ease.

8. **When head trash jumps back up again, that's okay. Quick tossing is easy.** Just close your eyes, step back into your de-stress trash room in front of the window, fill a bag and toss it.

## TOSS IT FASTER

After you have stepped up several times (the more the better), you can skip the fast breathing section and go directly to the room. When you decide to toss it, you can choose where to emerge on the method's timeline. You might decide to start by standing just outside the room's door or directly in front of the window.

Periodically, be sure to go back to the fast breathing step-up section. I like the fact that fast deep breathing has no autopilot and requires complete awareness.

## "TOSS OUT THE TRASH" QUICKSHIFT™

When something keeps gnawing at your mind:

1. **Close your eyes and take a deep, slow breath.** As you exhale, see yourself inside the clutter-free room.

2. **Walk over to window.** Grab a garbage bag and dump your head trash.

3. **Securely tie the bag and toss it out the wide open window.** Your head trash vanishes. Take a few moments to enjoy your peace of mind.

## PROGRESS CONFIRMATION

Since you've experienced your tenth MindShift Exercise™ Toss Out the Trash, I suggest you intentionally say the following aloud:

> *"I am further creating the life I want and de-cluttering my mind, now that I choose to Toss Out the Trash and release mental garbage in my de-stress trash room—a quiet place where I now find peace."*

## UP NEXT...

In the next chapter, you'll discover an unexpected meaning for *"F... me?"* You know how much I like word *play*.

The following is the most overlooked and undervalued action we can take to shift our mindset and change our life. An email from a 45-year-old, macho man told me this literally saved his life!

Read on and discover your eleventh MindShift Exercise™. I'm looking forward to hearing how *f'ing* might save your life, too.

# Chapter 15
# The Sound of Forgiveness (MSE 11)

*F... Me? No! F... You!*

Gotcha! I bet the F-word paused your reading for just a moment. Your head might have slightly moved in response. You might have squinted your eyes a bit. Yes, words are powerful.

Because of one of the biggest trigger words that cross language barriers, you might have flipped to this chapter before you read this far. But, this F-word is different than you might be thinking.

More than 80% of people look at chapters and content before they start reading a book. Then, many jump from one chapter to another, to get a flavor of the read.

Regardless of whether you cruised to this chapter or you just began your journey and started here, I want to point out that the most important *F-word* is *Forgive*. Your eleventh MindShift Exercise™ is *The Sound of Forgiveness.*

## DADDY STORY

Growing up, Dad was physically abusive and mean to me. Treating me like a dog, he slapped me around and told me to stay. He continually told me I was fat.

Since I was mentally fragile and highly sensitive, I thought I was fat, even though I was thin. I hated Dad because he saw no value in me.

This following "memory moment" was anchored by highly charged emotions and physical actions. I vividly recall the details:

I am fifteen and the same height as Dad at an even six feet. It's a hot summer afternoon. All I wanted to do was get away from Dad on the front porch.

When I turn to step off the porch, Dad forcefully grabs my left arm. I react. Spinning to my right, I lock my bent arms and clench my fists. My right elbow crashes into Dad's side. His ribs break and I quietly utter, "Never touch me again, or I will kill you!"

He physically left me alone after that. However, he continued to downgrade my self-worth.

Fast forward forty years. Driving across country on business, I'm listening to a Zig Ziglar recording where he's talking about the value of forgiveness. I've always referred to our vehicles as the *Rolling Universities*. In that moment, Zig took me to school, and I had a revelation.

Although I have no recollection of what exactly Zig said, in a flash I realized that the way Dad treated me had nothing to do with me. It was about him.

Thinking back while listening to Zig, I recalled a photograph of Dad that was taken when he was in high school and unable to serve during World War II. The picture was of his seven-player basketball team. He was standing in the back row, arms crossed, shoulders slumped, and head tilted over to the side. It was obvious that Dad totally lacked self-confidence as a teenager and felt less-than.

Because of the varicose veins in his legs, Dad had been rejected by the military. He was classified as 4-F by the Selective Service and deemed as unfit for military service. He was sent back to high school as a reject, which further downgraded his self-worth and likely formed one of the foundation pillars for his life.

As a father, he was just trying to be the commander of his life and find his value. He just didn't know how.

In that moment, I forgave Dad for treating me the way he did. I felt a huge weight lift off my shoulders and float upward. I literally saw a dark cloud disappear through the car's open sunroof.

The experience was more about forgiving me than forgiving Dad. I believe self-forgiveness is the most overlooked and undervalued action, one which changes the way we feel about ourselves. The action of self-forgiveness can potentially change anyone's life for the better.

## FORGIVING USING SOUND

As you know, our mind-body connection is real and continually flows—from mind to body, then from our body back to our mind —each influencing the other.

Over time, I've learned that the more we use particular body parts, including our five senses, the more our brain becomes involved. When more of our brain is involved doing additional tasks, our brain becomes occupied and automatically pulls our mind away from sadness, remorse, guilt, and even blame.

Often people use music to help them shift their mental attention and prepare for the day. Every morning, one of my coaching clients connects her smartphone to portable speakers and blasts away while she showers. The difference in the way she feels, before and after, clearly illustrates the positive impact of the music she likes.

In 2011, a team of Montreal researchers published a paper stating that listening to favorite music can trigger the release of dopamine into two distinct parts of our brain. As I mentioned earlier, dopamine is our body's *happy chemical*. The result is that we feel happy and want more. We literally crave more music.

When I discovered that the sound of music affects different areas of our brain, I started playing with sound tones. Eventually, using sound became another tool for your MindShift Toolbox™.

In *The Sound of Forgiveness*, you go through a vocal process by engaging multiple senses. Then, you speak lovingly to yourself.

- Use your voice to create vibrations caused by closing your mouth while saying the word "forgive" and feeling the specific tones.
- Say five short sentences out loud to yourself using your name. You will find these sentences later in the chapter.

Using word power, this process helps shift our *self-forgiveness gear*. For me, I kept grinding gears for years trying to forgive myself until I learned to play with words and tones. There is a part of me that wonders if this forgiveness method deals directly with frequencies—the vibrations and energy of thought—as brought to light by quantum physics. Maybe it does.

The concept that sound affects our mind-body health goes back thousands of years in ancient Eastern teachings, as well as in the healing power of Yoga. I am intrigued by the notion that we can use our voice and objects, like tuning forks and singing bowls, as sound therapy to shift the way we physically and mentally feel.

## REMINDER

If you have physical challenges, your body-mind connection can still work as long as you imagine you are going through the physical motions. If you are unable to speak or hear on any level, visualize that you are. In your mind, speak or hum a tone, and hear your voice.

Within *The Sound of Forgiveness* method, there are five sentences you say using your own name. Imagine you are intentionally saying those words.

If you are fully able to speak and hear, but wish to step into the self-forgiveness mode while in public without others hearing you, of course you can go through the process silently.

## PREPARE TO RELEASE

**Set Your Intention.** Once you have mastered the tuning method, you can initiate the process by repeating your intention statement over and over. Rather than speed-talk, say it with full intention. Focus on every word as you internally shift your mental gears from self-guilt to self-forgiveness.

Whatever you repeat continually can become your mantra. You might even want to sing-song the intention.

> *"My intention is to forgive myself and release that which no longer serves me."*

Repeatedly practicing any MindShift Exercise™ will speed up the process. Regularly doing any exercise is the fastest way to learn. By so doing, MindShifting can become second nature to you.

Yes, the simple process of forgiving yourself may at first seem odd to you, even out of place. For years, I resisted forgiving myself and felt like I did not deserve to be forgiven. That is clearly a *Pity Party*.

## CRITICIZE, FORGIVE OR SET ASIDE

I promise you this—you do deserve to forgive yourself. Once you learn how to forgive yourself, you can close your eyes and shift through the process smoothly. When you feel like you just made a mistake and instantly begin to blame yourself, you have several choices:

- Continue to criticize yourself.
- Fine-tune your mindset and begin to forgive yourself right away.
- Set aside a terrible mistake you just made and come back to the forgiveness process later. You have other priorities right now.

The "set-aside-process" frees up our mental powers, allowing us to shake off guilt and refocus on what is going on in that moment. Consciously put a reminder on your "come-back-here" list.

For me, I say to myself, *"I'm okay. Later, I will find my lesson and forgive myself for screwing up."*

Sure, self-forgiveness takes practice, but you are worth the investment of time. Otherwise, holding onto guilt and self-blame anchors the feelings of being less-than, and those thoughts will certainly take root and grow.

## IDENTIFY YOUR FORGIVENESS NEEDS

Pull up any situation where you wish to seek self-forgiveness, whether big or small. Think about an incident where you:

- Felt you had made a mistake.
- Blamed yourself and felt that action was unforgivable.
- Felt awful about something you had done.

**RATE IT BEFORE**

- **Baseline:** As you have done before, rate the situation you brought to mind. How do you feel? 0-10? Zero is where you are completely neutral and detached from self-blame, self-guilt, and self-judgment. The 10-rating is the worst, "Take me to the emergency room."

- **Finish Line:** When you finish, re-rate how you are feeling so you will have evidence that self-forgiveness is doable. How do you feel? 0-10?

- **Shift Results:** What is the difference? (Beginning baseline minus finish line.) If your rate-meter does not move, that is okay, too. Sometimes it takes several times to let go of what no longer serves us.

You may resist letting go. You might feel like you have too much invested in your job, in your relationships, in whatever you are doing right now. Sometimes the guilt monster grabs you by the throat, and you shout to yourself, *"There's simply no possible way I can afford to let go!"*

I've been there more times than I'd like to admit. When I flat out resisted letting go, life blindsided me and got my attention. I guess it's been life's way of schooling me. In the process, I've learned the value of unconditional self-forgiveness.

Let's begin.

**"THE SOUND OF FORGIVENESS" DETAILED STEPS**

**Step 1: Bring your guilty situation to mind.** Sit comfortably in a chair; put your feet flat on the floor. Take a deep, slow breath and exhale slowly, completely.

Life is about making decisions with incomplete information. Sometimes, our decisions are correct. Other times, our decisions are incorrect. That's okay. Take a moment to find some good in the situation where you believe you were wrong.

Look for the lessons within your mistake. That is what life is about—learning by living.

**Step 2: Take another slow, deep breath, and as you exhale, begin to forgive and let go.** With the intention of total self-forgiveness say, *"My intention is to forgive myself and release that which no longer serves me."*

The more heartfelt feelings you put into saying your intention, the more your subconscious begins to believe you are on the road to forgiving yourself. Let's call that *Intentional Tuning.*

**Step 3: Take another deep breath, and put your right hand over your heart.** As you slowly release the breath, say, *"I am preparing to forgive myself. I am preparing to forgive you, [your name]."*

By adding your name into the steps, you are personalizing the process. You are beginning to truly value who you are, regardless of what you have done, or how you doubt who you have become. Taking concrete action to forgive yourself is vital to activate your self-esteem.

**Step 4: Breathe deeply. As you exhale, say, "I for-give" and play with the "vvvvv" sound.** Hold the second syllable of the word *"for-give"* at the point where your mouth and teeth connect on the *"v-sound"*. Feel the vibration of the *"vvvvvv-sound"*.

Repeat *"I for-give"* again and feel the *"vvvvvvv"* vibrate your mouth, in your teeth, on your cheeks, and in the bones of the face.

**Step 5: As you continue saying "I for-give," visualize the "v's" morphing into wings.** The wings transform and whisk away guilt, judgment, and blame.

As the terrible trinity—guilt, judgment, and blame—rises up and begins to disappear, you are no longer stuck in the past. You are moving forward on your timeline to where you are now, to the place where you are reaffirming your value.

**Step 6: Breathe in deeply before you lovingly say out loud each of the five *release-sentences*.** Starting with "I'm sorry" is powerful. Saying those words to yourself begins to release your guilt, restore self-trust, and fortify your belief in your goodness and self-worth.

Ending each release-sentence with your name is a way of stepping into the mindful, self-compassion mode. Speaking these sentences out loud—being a self-talker—is an effective way to learn how to MindShift from self-despair to self-love.

As you talk your way through the sentences, begin to smile. By the end of the fifth sentence, you will be smiling from your heart and your soul. Feel that truth traveling throughout your body, reflected on your face and beaming through your eyes.

In essence, you can sweet-talk your way to self-forgiveness in an amazingly short time frame.

As you finish each sentence, fully exhale through softly pursed lips.

- *"I'm sorry, [your name]."*
- *"I forgive you, [your name]."*
- *"I love you, [your name]."*
- *"Thank you, [your name]."*
- *"You are forgiven, [your name]."*

**Step 7: Open your eyes and continue smiling. Look up to the right to access the creative side of your brain and ask...** Pivot your entire body 45 degrees to the right, continue looking upwards and ask, *"Why is it becoming so easy to forgive myself?"*

Pause for a moment. Breathe in and out softly. Allow the question to settle and float down into your subconscious. Your mind will continue answering a *properly-asked question*, which effectively gives your mind the power to rewrite your mental software code.

**Step 8: Continue looking slightly upward and smiling. Accessing your creativity, breathe, and ask...** Breathe in and sit up tall. Exhale, release and drop your shoulders. Smiling, finish by asking, *"Where would I rather be?"* Just sit quietly for a while.

As before, there is no need to reply. Your subconscious mind will do that job for you.

**Self-Forgiveness Feels Good.** You have now fully engaged the power of *The Sound of Forgiveness*. You are worthy and valuable. Self-forgiveness is empowering.

## RATE IT AFTER

Now that you are becoming adept at forgiving yourself, rate it. Compare your before and after numbers so you can see how your *Mindset Scale*™ changed.

- Where are you right now? How do you feel about what you brought to mind? 0-10?
- How did you rate your feelings before you engaged in the forgiveness process? 0-10?
- What is the difference?

When your after-number is smaller, you have evidence that you are fluidly moving towards self-forgiveness. If your after-number is the same, or even higher than the before-number, you might be struggling and continue to dwell on guilt. That's okay, too.

Sometimes we need to dig a bit deeper and unearth mental garbage. It took me years to realize I had created a mental landfill full of head trash. *Releasing that, which no longer serves me,* while forgiving me for hating on myself, continually transforms my life. You might experience the same rebirth.

When we continue to harbor self-judgment, we must learn how to shift our mindset quickly and forgive. This alone can neutralize the stress in our body, which helps to repair and renew our mind-body-spirit connection.

Just now, thinking about having a *mind-body disconnect,* brought to mind that stress can blow a circuit breaker in our body and interrupt the flow of energy. Stress can also create a short circuit, allowing energy to travel along unintended paths and harm multiple parts of our body.

## "THE SOUND OF FORGIVENESS" AT-A-GLANCE

1. **Sit comfortably in a chair; feet flat on the ground. Bring a guilty situation to mind and find the lessons.** Take a deep, slow breath and exhale slowly, completely.

2. **Take another slow, deep breath, and as you exhale, begin to forgive and let it go by intending to do so. Say...** *"My intention is to forgive myself and release that which no longer serves me."*

3. **Take another deep breath again, hand to heart.** As you slowly exhale, *"I am preparing to forgive myself. I am preparing to accept and forgive you, [your name]."*

4. **Breathe deeply. Exhale and say, "I for-give", holding and playing with the "vvvvv" sound.** Repeat, *"I for-give,"* again and feel the *"vvvvvvv"* vibrate throughout your head and within your mouth.

5. **As you continue saying "I for-give," visualize the "v's" morphing into wings.** The wings transform and whisk away your guilt, judgment and blame.

6. **Breathe in deeply before you lovingly say each of the five *release-sentences* out loud.** Smile as you talk your way through the process. Finish each and fully exhale through softly pursed lips.

   • *"I'm sorry, [your name]."*

   • *"I forgive you, [your name]."*

   • *"I love you, [your name]."*

   • *"Thank you, [your name]."*

   • *"You are forgiven, [your name]."*

7. **Open your eyes and continue smiling. Look up to the right.** Pivot your entire body 45 degrees to the right and ask, *"Why is it so easy to forgive myself?"*

8. **Continue looking slightly upward and smiling. Accessing your creativity, breathe in and sit up tall.** Exhale, release and drop your shoulders. Finish by asking, *"Where would I rather be?"*

The following is a shorthand forgiveness process you can do in less than 90 seconds. It might take much longer to read through the steps than to do in real time.

## "THE SOUND OF FORGIVENESS" QUICKSHIFT™

Rather than forgo using the 8-step method, use all the At-A-Glance steps to fully engage and activate self-forgiveness. Once you have fully mastered *The Sound of Forgiveness*, keep this QuickShift™ handy in your toolbox as well.

1. **Close your eyes. Hand to heart.** Take a few moments breathing in deeply and exhaling slowly and completely. Feel your hand resting in your heart's energy field. See love flowing from your hand to your heart, mending any energetic fractures, soothing and healing your feelings of guilt. As you remain in the midst of your mind-body-spirit connection influence, spend a few moments thinking about a lesson you are in the process of learning.

2. **Breathe deeply. As you exhale slowly, release guilt and say, "I for-give," continually holding the "v... vvvvvvv".** In your mind's eye, envision the "v's" turning into the wings on your guilt-words and fly away. Continue breathing in and out deeply, as you say, feel, see, and hear the *v-sound*. You have now engaged multiple senses, which give tasks to different parts of your brain.

3. **Breathe in and out slowly as you lovingly take each self-forgiveness step by saying:** *"I'm sorry, [your name]. I forgive you, [your name]. I love you, [your name]. Thank you, [your name]. You are forgiven, [your name]."*

## PROGRESS CONFIRMATION

Since you've experienced your eleventh MindShift Exercise™ *The Sound of Forgiveness*, this journey is nearly complete. I suggest you intentionally say the following aloud:

> *"Gratefully, I am creating the life I love, now that I can gently shift into the self-forgiveness gear, neutralize body stress, and fine-tune my mindset with The Sound of Forgiveness."*

## UP NEXT...

In the next chapter, you'll discover the simple key to finding your authentic self—who you truly are. Rather than continually seeking confirmation from outside worldly standards that verify you are valuable, you must look inside and stop blaming yourself for failing.

Within your twelfth and final MindShift Exercise™ inside this book, I want you to literally hear my voice speaking directly to you... for I love you, just the way you are.

# Chapter 16
# Release the Guilt (MSE 12)

Self-forgiveness is a huge step in the quest to unearth your authentic self—who you truly are. Hopefully, in a short time, you will have begun to faithfully practice forgiving yourself. In so doing, self-forgiveness becomes natural and second nature. That way, you can look back and learn from your experiences without holding onto guilt.

Yet, releasing guilt is often the biggest handicap for many people. To help remedy that, your twelfth and final MindShift Exercise™ in this book is *Release the Guilt.*

Life has taught me that when we hold onto guilt, we are our own worst enemy. I've been at the top of the class "hating" myself and devaluing my efforts.

When I think, *"My writing is just not good enough,"* my *Energetic Radar Tags* me. My ego reacts, *"Crap, I did that again!"* Automatically shifting brings to mind, *"That's okay. Time to let that go."*

After a brief pause, I breathe deeply and shift to self-forgiveness. Or, I might mentally hop to the *De-stress Room and Toss that Head Trash*. Releasing guilt automatically comes along for the ride.

## DETACHED VS PASSIVE OBSERVER

Throughout, I have dwelled on the importance of being a detached observer rather than fueling internal strife, but I wanted to clarify one more thing:

> *Being a detached observer is dramatically different from being a passive observer, where we do just that... observe and do nothing else.*

Detachment allows us to observe, and then, take proactive action. When we learn lessons from experiences rather than wallow in failure, we become the *doer* rather than the *don'ter*.

- When we stay attached to the outcome, we allow our emotions and guilt to distort our life's story from a life-of-learning to a continually-failing-saga.

- By taking action and re-framing whatever happens in our life—*by pondering and chewing on that for a while before we toss out the head trash*—we heighten self-awareness through persistent, gutsy self-exploration.

Frankly, I took a leap of faith by sharing my MindShift Exercises™ with you. Initially, I was reluctant and attached to the outcome—fearful the methods might feel a bit "out there."

Rather than being New Age concepts, what I am passing on is ageless. *Conscious, energetic shifting* has veritable roots going back over 5,000 years!

## PROOF

Here's a fact. I asked for proof that my MindShift Exercises™ work and got exactly what I asked for with my stroke in 2013. MindShifting helped reroute many of my brain's neural pathways in three short days. The proof I had been seeking appeared.

Some of my word-mental-files are still hiding. When I'm stuck on a word, rather than say or think, *"I forgot,"* I still say to myself, *"I temporarily mislaid that word"* [as mentioned in Chapter 1].

In addition, I now add a properly-asked question to the shift, *"Where is THAT word hiding?"*

Asking the subconscious mind to help locate a misplaced word is a lot like opening an Internet browser and placing a search. I wonder if I can speed up the process by telling my mind to *"just Google it."*

When words seemed to slip my mind in the months after my stroke, I was frustrated and a frown flashed across my face. Releasing the guilty feeling has been both positive and profound.

Today, I describe a word by defining it to whoever is listening. When they willingly help me locate that word, I'm grateful and always smile.

In fact, I have *temporally mislaid words* during coaching sessions, webinars, and while speaking in front of audiences. Once I locate the word, I literally go through the process of physically anchoring that word then and there.

Using my personal anchoring-tool, I smile and tap on my left wrist with two fingers while I consciously say the misplaced word six times. In lieu of rapidly repeating the word, I use the word in logical sentences and phrases while mentally seeing the word.

The process is similar to memory tricks that help us recall anything. Usually, that re-discovered word has now found its new word folder and been filed away for easy access.

## HOW WE LEARN

When I became a certified consultant in the '80s using a personality profile system, I discovered people learn differently. Each of us has a dominant learning style, but *no single way is the only correct way.*

Consider what your dominant learning style might be:

- *Visual learner* learns by seeing, by reading, by watching.
- *Auditory learner* learns easier by listening, by hearing, by speaking.
- *Kinesthetic learner* learns by physically engaging, by touching, by doing.

Regardless of how we naturally learn, when we challenge ourselves and move out of our comfort zone by engaging different senses, we learn and retain more. You can add MindShifting skills to your memory banks by using multiple senses.

On top of that, reflecting is clearly the *anchoring tool* that adds what we just experienced to our long-term memory. I believe many people overlook contemplating while continuing to cram, just like burning the midnight oil during exam week. Unfortunately, I have done that much of my life.

## WHY SEEK AUTHENTICITY

In short, when we live life from our authentic self, we are genuinely grounded. We find our balance and tap into our strength, rather than giving energy to our mistakes and repeating them. We can then be true to ourselves and decisively take action.

The intention of finding our authentic self clearly empowers us so that we can confidently proceed:

- Pinpoint what we do well, so we can repeat that process and excel at whatever we do.

- Discover our stumbling blocks, so we can side step, ponder, then clear the field.

- Focus our energy, so we can sustain, grow, and transform.

## RINSE AND REPEAT

Over time, I discovered that setting the tone for group coaching sessions needed to start with the same words. In the beginning, I thought it was good enough to simply state something once when a client began coaching.

Eventually, it became obvious that it takes time for people to internalize new concepts. It took me years to learn simple truths. Some people never seem to get it.

After eighteen months, a coaching client suddenly said, "Detach and observe! I finally get it. Your words finally sunk in."

Statistically, in order to learn anything, we have to experience what we want to learn six times. Regardless of the primary way we learn—by seeing, hearing or doing—using various ways helps us learn faster.

At first, having to repeat everything six times before it sunk in gave me another knee jerk reaction. Eventually, I embraced the concept as a way to forgive myself for taking a lot of time to learn anything.

With that said, I am finishing this book with one intention: *To help you find your authentic self—uniquely and perfectly you.*

To accomplish that I'm also giving you a bundle of *Mental Focus Truths* plus a MindShift Exercise™ that is my way of reaching out and holding you in my arms. My hope is that you will use these truths to find and stay your authentic path. Consider making the truths a part of your daily MindShifting ritual.

These truths also help me be grateful for who I am and what I pass on to you. And, yes you have seen some of these truths several times throughout the book, especially referencing *"the words we choose."*

The bottom line: We often must experience a concept multiple times before it finally sinks in... just like anchoring a recovered misplaced-word.

## MENTAL FOCUS TRUTHS

1. The way we ask ourselves questions is critical.

2. The words we choose will set ourselves up for either success or failure.

3. At any point in time, we have a choice of being in judgment or acceptance.

4. Judgment produces guilt and reaction.

5. Acceptance produces lessons and allows growth.

6. Above all, our intention is to remain detached and observe, because the mere act of consciously observing creates change.

## "RELEASE THE GUILT" DETAILS

Just prior to a group coaching session by way of a webinar, I decided to add visual learning into the process. To do so, I put together a graphic for *Release the Guilt.* My intention was to reach out, hold my clients in my arms, and help them let their guilt go.

## PICTURES SPEAK VOLUMES

During the group session, I shared the graphic on the screen. Immediately after the session, the following phone text arrived from a client, "Today's exercise saved my friend's life!"

My client had received a phone call during the session from a close friend, who was suicidal. Muting the computer's audio, my client stayed visually connected and read the exercise to her friend. Her friend said she felt an immediate shift, released guilt, and was at peace.

You'll find the graphic in your bonus bundle. I included different sizes you can print out: either to take with you or to post on your wall. Some people have touched my heart by using this graphic as their smartphone lock screen.

Be sure to go to my personal website and ask for the bonus, which includes MindShifting audios, graphics, and checklists: **www.DonnaBlevins.com/mindshift**

## "RELEASE THE GUILT" TRANSCRIPT

*Donna Blevins speaking:*

> "*Close your eyes and take a deep cleansing, restful breath. Exhale with a deep sigh... Aahhhh...*
>
> *At this moment, I am giving you a soul-healing hug. I am wrapping you in my arms. Feel it.*
>
> *Rest your head on my chest and allow yourself to lean into my arms.*
>
> *Your cares are going away. The stress is leaving your body.*
>
> *Take another deep, restful breath. As you exhale, release any residue of guilt, judgment, and blame.*

*Now smile as you feel the calm... the peacefulness. For you are perfect, just the way you are."*

By converting the graphic into QuickShift™ Steps, it fits nicely in the Rolodex section in the Appendix at the back of the book.

## "RELEASE THE GUILT" QUICKSHIFT™

**Donna Blevins:** *"Hear my voice as I speak directly to you and hold you in my arms."*

1. **Close your eyes. Breathe deeply and exhale with a sigh...** *"Aahhh."*

2. **Feel my arms wrapping completely around you.** I am giving you a heartfelt, soul-healing hug.

3. **Rest your head on my chest.** Lean into my arms. Feel your cares and stress leaving your body.

4. **Take another deep, restful breath and release.** As you exhale, release any remaining residue of guilt, judgment, and blame.

5. **Smile. Feel the calm flow over you.** You are fully at peace.

6. **You are valuable, worthy and perfect...** *just the way you are.*

## PROGRESS CONFIRMATION

*Hurrah!* Since you are the driver and chose to travel with me throughout the book, you've now experienced your twelfth MindShift Exercise™ *Release the Guilt.*

Anchor the process of releasing guilt that suddenly jumps up, stresses you, and assaults your mind, body, and spirit. Create the nurturing habit of *intentionally* saying the following:

> *"Thankfully, I am taking control of my mind and creating the life I love, now that I am letting go of guilt, judgment, and blame with Release the Guilt, and acknowledging that I am perfect, just the way I am."*

## UP NEXT...

Life's journey continues. As I've said time and time again, learning is a continual process rather than being once-and-done. Everyone's a work in progress. The choice is in your hands.

When you clearly set your intention to develop the habit of MindShifting at a moment's notice—*at the drop of a dime*—you can become the master of your emotions, your thoughts, and your life. Otherwise, you will remain the bystander, and let your emotions control you while life passes you by.

*You do have the power to create the life you want by choosing what you do.*

*You can choose how you look at life, where you focus, and how you shift. Shifting your perspective is the key to re-framing your reality.*

As you continue to practice and master shifting your mindset, people will begin asking you, "Why are you so happy? What are you on? I want some of that!"

Give them some more of that.

You are taking control of your life by being the driver. I am profoundly grateful and extremely proud of you for stepping up and taking the wheel.

Now, shift away and tell me how MindShifting changed your life! I look forward to hearing from you when you grab your bundles of thank you gifts here: **www.DonnaBlevins.com/mindshift**

One more thing. I'd appreciate you posting a review of this book on Amazon and telling a friend. You can also reach out to me on Facebook or Twitter: **@BigGirlPoker**

# APPENDIX
## MINDSHIFT EXERCISE™ ROLODEX

# Appendix
## MindShift Exercise™ Rolodex

In essence, an old-fashioned Rolodex is an address book on a wheel. When I was in real estate in the '80s and '90s, I kept three huge ones on my desk and referenced them every day, even after becoming an avid computer user.

Turning a Rolodex wheel, I'd find a person's name, their address, phone number, what they did, or facts about their family. I made notes about a person and what they liked and disliked. That way, I could personalize my contact with them.

Here, within your MindShift Rolodex, is the place you can go to fine-tune your connection with each of the twelve MindShift Exercises™ (MSE). You'll also find a reference back to the chapter where each method was introduced and explained in detail. Voila! You now have its address!

## MIND-BODY INNER-CONNECTION

Practice generates muscle and mindset memory. Repetition trains both your body and your mind while strengthening the union between your mind-body connection.

## ANCHOR

At the end of each MindShift Exercise™ you'll find its *Progress Confirmation*, specifically designed to help that method take root and become a natural part of you. Intentionally saying each *Progress Confirmation* aloud further anchors that method deep within your subconscious mind. Rather than speed-talk, speak with full intention as you focus on every word.

## "GEAR UP"
## Location: Chapter 2

**RECAP:** *Gear Up* is graceful and has two, simple QuickShift™ steps. In one short breath, you are aware. You become the driver rather than remaining an unwitting passenger.

**"GEAR UP" QUICKSHIFT™**

1. **Slowly take one deep breath as you close your eyes and visualize you're sitting in the driver's seat.** Hold your breath as you reach over and intentionally grasp your gearshift.

2. **Slowly exhale. In that one single breath, you've become aware.** By doing so, you've experienced a true reality shift. You are now back in control of your mind in a mere moment.

**Added benefit:** Using the clutch-shift intuitive process, found in Chapter 2, combines physical movement with mental intention. When you integrate mentally-seeing with physically-doing, MindShifting clearly speeds up. The process is so fast, you can shift your mindset during one single, long deep breath. However, loitering in the calm for a dozen slow, deep belly breaths is heartwarming and soul soothing.

## PROGRESS CONFIRMATION

> *"I am taking control of my mind, now that I have learned to shift with Gear Up and become the driver."*

## "HMM...ISN'T THAT INTERESTING?"
### Location: Chapter 4

**RECAP:** *Hmm... Isn't That Interesting?* helps you shift away from fear in a mere instant. This method can also be used to shift away from pain, remorse, guilt, self-judgment, and loss of love.

## "HMM... ISN'T THAT INTERESTING?" QUICKSHIFT™

When stress, conflict, frustration, or anger arises, take two intentional breaths paired with subtle body movements.

1. **Take a deep breath, smile, nod slightly and say, "Hmm... isn't that interesting?"** In the moment you become aware, you detach and stop fueling chaos. In public, "Hmm" to yourself by clearing your throat and thinking the words.

2. **Take another deep breath, smile and continue nodding as you look up and to the right. Ask, "Where would I rather be?"** You gave your subconscious mind a well-crafted question to begin shifting on a deeper level.

**Added benefit:** The 7-step process, found in Chapter 4, combines ten powerful actions in real time—forgiving, envisioning, creating, body engagement, noticing, detaching, observing, speaking, looking, and asking. The method reduces stress on multiple levels!

## PROGRESS CONFIRMATION

> *"I am creating the life I want, now that I have become the detached observer with 'Hmm...Isn't That Interesting?' and asked the 'Where' question that delivers code modifiers to my subconscious mind."*

## "90-SECOND SHIFT"
### Location: Chapter 6

**RECAP:** Breathing is a balancing and energizing tool. When you breathe and count to yourself, there's an unexpected sweet spot that helps embed this technique as a positive habit. Pick the in-and out-counts that are comfortable. Set your goal to exhale to a count that is twice as long as you inhaled.

## "90-SECOND SHIFT" QUICKSHIFT™

1. **Get comfortable.** Close your eyes, sit comfortably, and relax your shoulders.

2. **Notice the air moving as you breathe: In to 6, out to 12.** Count in your mind and "see" the numbers. As you inhale through your nose, count to 6. As you slowly exhale through softly, pursed lips, count to 12.

3. **Smile when you finish.** Notice how much better you feel.

**Added benefits:** Add this mighty-MINI to your all-around, mental preparation ritual before, and while you are doing, anything. Think of this asset as a "reset, reboot, re-framing" tool. There is also an unexpected mind-body connection surrounding breathing: Inhaling activates certain parts of your body while exhaling can literally settle your entire being.

## PROGRESS CONFIRMATION

> "Now that I have learned how to gently reboot with the 90-Second Shift, I am taking control of my mind and my body."

## "ENERGETIC RADAR"
### Location: Chapter 7

**RECAP:** We all can catch energetic flu from the sludge around us and from our own heartless self-judgment. Once you install your *Energetic Radar*, you receive alerts as your energy shifts to negativity. Once aware, your perspective instantly shifts. You are back in control rather than remaining life's puppet.

## "ENERGETIC RADAR" QUICKSHIFT™

1. **Close your eyes. Breathe deeply as you lovingly hold your *Energetic Radar* Governor in your hands.** Flip the switch to OFF, then back to ON, just as you would with an electric circuit breaker.

2. **Tap five times on any preferred spot on your body.** You've now installed, activated, and paired your *Energetic Radar* with your mind.

3. **Forgive yourself when your *Energetic Radar* alerts you that you're asleep at the wheel.** Upshift. Detach and observe. Decide your best action with the information you have, and take action.

**Added benefits:** The QuickShift™ is also a way to swiftly reconnect if you sense your *Energetic Radar* has short-circuited or disconnected.

## PROGRESS CONFIRMATION

> *"I am taking control of my mind and creating an uplifted life, now that I have installed and engaged my Energetic Radar to alert me when internal energy shifts in the wrong direction."*

## "TAG"
## Location: Chapter 8

**RECAP:** *Tag* is a loving, gentle way to trigger a positive MindShift by changing your words. Every self-defeating word is a ticking time bomb. Unfortunately, we rarely examine our word choice by listening to the words as they come out of our mouth or even considering whether our words are positive or negative before we speak. *Tagging* yourself is a forgiving trigger.

## "TAG" QUICKSHIFT™

1. **Breathe, smile, *Tag*, and forgive.** When negative words jump out of your mouth, or negative thoughts drop into your mind, breathe in and smile. As you exhale, lovingly say "Tag" to yourself and drop your shoulders. Forgiveness flows throughout your body.

2. **Take your time to locate kind, forgiving words.** Re-phrase what you said or what just came to mind.

**Added Benefits:** For your convenience, *Tag* is also your *Energetic Radar Plug-in* and will help widen your radar's field. You are now aware when your energy dips. You are armed with a tool to tweak-your-speak or modify your spoken words.

## PROGRESS CONFIRMATION

> *"I am further taking control of my mind and creating the life I want, now that I have added Tag to my MindShift Toolbox™, which helps me monitor and shift away from negative thoughts and self-defeating words."*

## "SHIFT INTO NEUTRAL"
### Location: Chapter 9

**RECAP:** *Shift Into Neutral* has become my handy-on-the-go-tool that is just a thought away. The technique is simple, direct, and a great way to center yourself. When aware, this method gives you the ability to neutralize your negative mindset, and in concert, take a mental vacation.

## "SHIFT INTO NEUTRAL" QUICKSHIFT™

1. **Close your eyes and breathe deeply. Level ground.** Safe. Reach over and shift into neutral.

2. **Gently grasp your hair.** Lift up and open your spine.

3. **Connect the Golden Cord.** Upward into the Universe and plugged deep within the earth.

4. **Settle into your calm.** Rest there idling WITHIN neutral as you recharge your batteries.

**Added Benefits:** By practicing often and fully grasping the concept of settling INTO neutral, you create a healthy habit, neutralize the stress in your body, and help to refocus your mind.

The 9-step process in Chapter 9 is deliberately thoughtful. After the process becomes natural, consider shifting directly into neutral using only two steps #1 and #4 from the QuickShift™ above.

## PROGRESS CONFIRMATION

> *"I am taking time for myself and creating the life I want, now that I can naturally Shift Into Neutral to counter-balance negativity while taking a mental vacation and recharging my batteries."*

## "BLOW THE BULLY AWAY"
### Location: Chapter 10

**RECAP:** When someone bullies us, we give them authority over us by slipping into the victim mindset. That's where bullies get their power—*from us!* When you see yourself as the victim, you become the victim. You vacate the driver's seat and turn the wheel over to the bully.

## "BLOW THE BULLY AWAY" QUICKSHIFT™

1. **Bully is in your hand.** "It" is shrinking.

2. **Detach** and observe "it".

3. **Send love** from your heart to "its" heart.

4. **Huff & puff.** Blow "it" away.

**Added Benefits:** Notice the "it" within the QuickShift™. By simply revising how you notice "him, her, them, everyone, or even life" to "it, its, or itself", your WordShift™ dethrones the bully as well.

The 8-step method in Chapter 10 is empowering as you engage both your body and your mind. For many, the direct effect of this method is uplifting and surprisingly swift.

## PROGRESS CONFIRMATION

*"I am creating the life I want, now that I have sidestepped being the victim, stopped bullying myself and learned how to lovingly Blow the Bully Away."*

## "THE EGG"
Location: Chapter 12

**RECAP:** *The Egg* insulates yourself from external negative energy, while allowing perfectly aligned, loving energy to flow continually to you. The outside mirrored surface is selective, deflecting negativity out into the cosmos where that dark energy becomes neutralized.

## "THE EGG" MAINTENANCE QUICKSHIFT™

1. **Close your eyes. Take one slow, deep breath. Exhale and detach.** Physically move and look around. Notice any *Egg* cracks or fractures.

2. **Inhale deeply; slowly move hands up your core to the sky.** Palms facing inward, then upward, collecting energy. Arms reaching towards the sky. Hands fully charged.

3. **As you exhale, palms facing outward, slowly sweep your hands downward in a full arc to your side.** Perfectly aligned healing energy is collected, received, and absorbed.

**Added Benefits:** Using the 7-step method in Chapter 12, you identify and *Put Your Egg On* through physical movement and intentional visioning. Using the QuickShift™, in two deep breaths coupled with deliberate movement, you locate and intentionally smooth over *Egg* fractures while energizing self.

## PROGRESS CONFIRMATION

> *"I am taking control of my mind and creating the life I want, now that I have put on my flexible, mirrored Egg, which completely surrounds my energy field, deflects negativity, while allowing positive energy to flow through to me."*

## "PIT STOP"
### Location: Chapter 13

**RECAP:** *Pit Stop* is a fast and effective way to fuel up, change your focus, and recharge your batteries. You have your very own, built-in, pit crew at your fingertips—IN YOUR HANDS.

## "PIT STOP" QUICKSHIFT™

You can visualize this process within your mind's eye. However, when physically able to move, take action and fully activate your body-mind connection.

1. **Close your eyes and forgive yourself.** Take a deep forgiving breath. As you exhale, release the guilt.

2. **Hug yourself and light your fire!** Gently sway from side to side, smiling and giving thanks for who you are. Briskly rub your arms six times.

3. **Inhale deeply. Stroke hands diagonally across body and down to the side.** Exhale forcefully. Flick fingers sharply, releasing negative residue. Shake hands vigorously.

## PROGRESS CONFIRMATION

> *"I am taking full control of my mind and loving who I am, now that I come first and faithfully take me-time for a Pit Stop; using the power in the palm of my hands, I body-polish to repair and energize, hug myself and give thanks."*

## "TOSS THE TRASH"
### Location: Chapter 14

**RECAP:** *Toss the Trash* is a surprisingly fun way to get rid of head trash that continually surfaces.

## "TOSS OUT THE TRASH" QUICKSHIFT™

When something keeps gnawing at your mind:

1. **Close your eyes and take a deep, slow breath.** As you exhale, see yourself inside the clutter-free room.

2. **Walk over to window.** Grab a garbage bag and dump your head trash.

3. **Securely tie the bag and toss it out the wide open window.** Your head trash vanishes. Take a few moments to enjoy your peace of mind.

**Added Benefits:** The 8-step version in Chapter 14 uses controlled, fast breathing—*in, fast and deep… out, fast and complete*—which is very different than the controlled, slow way we usually breathe during MindShifting. Many people find controlled, fast breathing empowering while being cleansing.

## PROGRESS CONFIRMATION

> *"I am further creating the life I want and de-cluttering my mind, now that I choose to Toss Out the Trash and release mental garbage in my de-stress trash room—a quiet place where I now find peace."*

## "THE SOUND OF FORGIVENESS"
### Location: Chapter 15

RECAP: *The Sound of Forgiveness* fine-tunes your mindset. Even though self-forgiveness takes practice, you are well worth the investment of time. Otherwise, when you hold onto guilt and self-blame, you take ownership of those thoughts and feelings.

## "THE SOUND OF FORGIVENESS" QUICKSHIFT™

1. **Close your eyes. Hand to heart.** Breathe in deeply. Exhale slowly, completely. Love flows from hand to heart; mends energetic fractures; begins to heal shame and guilt.

2. **Breathe deeply. Exhale slowly. Release guilt and say, "I for-give," continually holding the "v…vvvvvvv".** In your mind's eye, envision the "v's" turning into the wings on your guilt-words and fly away.

3. **Breathe in and out slowly. Lovingly take each self-forgiveness step by saying:** *"I'm sorry, [your name]. I forgive you, [your name]. I love you, [your name]. Thank you, [your name]. You are forgiven, [your name]."*

Added Benefits: In the 8-step method in Chapter 15, you use a vocal process that engages multiple senses. You speak lovingly to self in a way that activates and nurtures self-forgiveness. The QuickShift™ shorthand forgiveness-process takes less than 90 seconds.

## PROGRESS CONFIRMATION

> *"Gratefully, I am creating the life I love, now that I can gently shift into the self-forgiveness gear, neutralize body stress, and fine-tune my mindset with The Sound of Forgiveness."*

## "RELEASE THE GUILT"
### Location: Chapter 16

**RECAP:** As you read through *Release the Guilt*, hear my voice inside your head and feel my arms wrap around you. Regardless of how much physical distance lies between us, we are energetically connected on a cellular level. My intention is for healing energy and light to flow through me and to you, helping you release guilt, self-judgment, and shame.

## "RELEASE THE GUILT" QUICKSHIFT™

1. **Close your eyes. Breathe deeply and exhale with a sigh...** "Aahhh."

2. **Feel my arms wrapping completely around you.** I am giving you a heartfelt, soul-healing hug.

3. **Rest your head on my chest.** Lean into my arms. Feel your cares and stress leaving your body.

4. **Take another deep, restful breath and release.** As you exhale, release any remaining residue of guilt, judgment, and blame.

5. **Smile. Feel the calm flow over you.** You are fully at peace.

6. **You are worthy and perfect...** just the way you are.

## PROGRESS CONFIRMATION

> *"Thankfully, I am taking control of my mind and creating the life I love, now that I am letting go of guilt, judgment and blame with Release the Guilt, and acknowledging that I am perfect, just the way I am."*

## SUMMARY

## YOUR MINDSHIFT ROLODEX IS COMPLETE!

Remember, the MindShift Rolodex is your go-to place for all twelve MindShift Exercises™, where each is recapped and summarized.

For each method, you'll also find its QuickShift™, Progress Confirmation statement, and reference back to the specific chapter where it is explained in detail.

I'm looking forward to hearing which MindShift Exercises™ are working well for you, how MindShifting might have changed your life, what I might have done differently, and where you would like me to focus going forward.

Be sure to take action and download your bundle of thank you gifts here: **www.DonnaBlevins.com/mindshift**

Take some time and savor how your MindShift Toolbox™ is coming together. The steering wheel is in your hands!

Also, please take a moment and post a review of this book on Amazon. I am profoundly grateful for you staying with me throughout this journey.

# About the Author

Donna Blevins wears many hats, but the one she is most proud of is "Coach." She has spent a lifetime studying the human mind and human potential, and in 2015, she earned her PhD in Metaphysical Coaching at an interfaith theological seminary. Dr. Blevins has appeared in "Who's Who and Why of Successful Florida Women," and is a proud recipient of the Recognition Award from the Department of Veterans Affairs.

Donna lives on the Gulf Coast of Florida with her four dogs, her Mama Peggy, and her husband Gregory.

For information on Donna's speaking, workshops, and coaching, please visit her Website at: **www.DonnaBlevins.com**

# Thanks to the Sponsor

This book was made possible by platinum sponsor-partner, Genesis Gaming Solutions Inc., the creator of the free mobile app, BRAVO® Poker Live, which keeps players up-to-date with the latest poker room information, promotions, and much more.

Donna Blevins:

> *"BRAVO® Poker Live is poker information on steroids—what's happening in real time, right now! The app is a responsive mobile app that is a breeze to use. It has always helped me shift my mindset on a dime about where and what I want to play.*
>
> *"You can check out the current live action and tournaments in your local card rooms or see what's happening worldwide. It's linked directly into the BRAVO® poker room management system used in card rooms and shows you what games are being spread and how many people are on the waiting list. If you're a serious poker player, or you just want to have fun, you must use this app!"*

## User Friendly

You can easily customize your own display to see what is currently going on at your favorite poker room. Or, you can access information on casino or card rooms within the preferred distance from you by using GPS or by entering a zip code. You can find specific Live Games by searching game and limit requirements, and tournaments can be searched by both date and buy-in.

BRAVO® Poker Live continues to deliver convenience to the poker playing community. Recent upgrades to the system include ground-breaking new features such as Online Waiting List Sign-Up and Online Pre-Registration, enabling users to reserve seats and buy-in remotely in advance.

Donna Blevins:

> *"We've been waiting a long time for the ability to sign up on a waiting list for a game and pre-register for a tournament without having to wait in a long line!"*

## FREE Download

The BRAVO® Poker LIVE mobile app is available for your iPhone, iPad, and Android mobile devices. In fact, you can even access the app on your desktop using any Internet browser here: **www.BravoPokerLive.com.**

# TITLES OF RELATED INTEREST
### Presented by Donna Blevins, PhD

## WORKSHOPS & CONSULTATION

**Visual & Image Projections:** Refine Your Brand and Skyrocket Sales

**Personal Profile Training:** Improves Work Productivity, Teamwork and Communication

**Table Image:** 21st Century Advanced Poker Tells

**MindShifting Made Easy:** The Keys to Shifting Your Mindset and Playing the Cards Life Deals

**Big Profits in Real Estate:** Buy and Sell Your Own Without Paying Commission

**Home Prescription®:** Today's Sure Cure for Selling Homes...Fast!

## TRAINING & COACHING HYBRID

**Poker Pure and Simple™:** Stay-At-Home Poker Boot Camp Coupled With Virtual LIVE Group Coaching

**10-Minutes-a-Day MindShift Magic:** 40-Day Action Plan That Puts You in Control of Your Mind

**Executive Coaching:** Customized Intuitive and Pragmatic Interface, In Person and Virtually

Do you have a headache trying to find a speaker, mindset coach or consultant? Then, take two aspirins and email Donna right away: Donna@DonnaBlevins.com

# Notes

# Notes